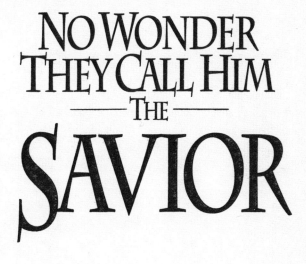

NO WONDER THEY CALL HIM THE SAVIOR

This Billy Graham Evangelistic Association
special edition is published with permission
from Questar.

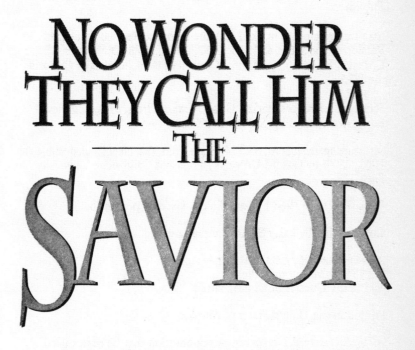

NO WONDER THEY CALL HIM THE SAVIOR

MAX LUCADO

Unless otherwise indicated, all Scripture references are from the Holy Bible: New International Version © 1973, 1978, 1984, by the International Bible Society. Used by persmission of Zondervan Bible Publishers.

Scripture references marked RSV are from the Revised Standard Version of the Bible, © 1946, 1952, 1971, 1973, Division of Christian Education , National Council of the Churches of Christ in the USA.

Scripture references marked Good News are from the Good News Bible; American Bible Society © 1976.

Scripture references marked NEB are from The New English Bible © 1961, 1970 by Oxford University Press and Cambridge University Press.

"The Boxer" © 1968 by Paul Simon. Used by permission.

Cover design by Larry Smith & Associates

NO WONDER THEY CALL HIM THE SAVIOR
© 1986 by Multnomah Press,
part of the Questar publishing family

Printed in the United States of America.

Library of Congress Cataloging-in-Publication Data

Lucado, Max
    No wonder they call him the Savior.

    1. Jesus Christ—Passion—Meditation.   I. Title.
BT431.L79   1986   232.9'6   85-31026
ISBN 0-913367-55-9

95 96 - 30 29

To Denalyn

with love eternal

CONTENTS

PART III   THE CROSS: ITS WISDOM

ACKNOWLEDGMENTS

A warm thank you to:

Dr. Tom Olbricht—for showing me what matters.

Dr. Carl Brecheen—for seeds planted in a hungry heart.

Jim Hackney—for your insights into our Master's sufferings.

Janine, Sue, Doris, and Paul—for your typing and encouragement.

Bob and Elsie Forcum—for your partnership in the gospel.

Randy Mayeux and Jim Woodroof—for your constructive comments and brotherly support.

Liz Heaney and Multnomah Press—for your keen editorial skills and creativity.

And most of all to Jesus Christ—please accept this offering of gratitude.

THE PART
THAT MATTERS

"I just want to know what counts." Deep Irish brogue. Dark, deep eyes. The statement was sincere. "Don't talk to me of religion, I've been down that road. And please, stay off theology. I have a degree in that. Get to the heart of it, okay? I want to know what counts."

His name was Ian. He was a student at a Canadian university where I was visiting. Through a series of events he found out I was a Christian and I found out he wanted to be but was disenchanted.

"I grew up in the church," he explained. "I wanted to go into the ministry. I took all the courses, the theology, the languages, the exegesis. But I quit. Something just didn't click."

"It's in there somewhere," he spoke with earnestness. "At least I think it is."

I looked up from my coffee as he began to stir his. Then he summarized his frustration with one question.

"What *really* matters? What counts? Tell me. Skip the periphery. Go to the essence. Tell me the part that matters."

The part that matters.

I looked at Ian for a long time. The question hung in the air. What should I have said? What could I have said? I could have told him about church. I could've given him a doctrinal answer or read him something classic like the twenty-third psalm, "The Lord is my shepherd . . ." But that all seemed too small. Maybe some thoughts on sexuality or prayer or the Golden Rule. No, Ian wanted the treasure—he wanted the meat.

Stop and empathize for a second. Can you hear his question? Can you taste his frustration? "Don't give me religion," he was saying. "Give me what matters."

What does matter?

In your Bible of over a thousand pages, what matters? Among all the do's and don'ts and shoulds and shouldn'ts, what is essential? What is indispensable? The Old Testament? The New? Grace? Baptism?

What would you have said to Ian? Would you have spoken on the evil of the world or maybe the eminence of heaven? Would you have quoted John 3:16 or Acts 2:38 or maybe read 1 Corinthians 13?

What really matters?

You've probably wrestled with this question. Maybe you've gone through the acts of religion and faith and yet found yourself more often than not at a dry well. Prayers seem empty. Goals seem unthinkable. Christianity becomes a warped record full of highs and lows and off-key notes.

Is this all there is? Sunday attendance. Pretty songs. Faithful tithings. Golden crosses. Three-piece suits. Big choirs. Leather Bibles. It is nice and all, but . . . where is the heart of it?

I stirred my coffee. Ian stirred his. I had no answer. All my verses so obediently memorized seemed inappropriate. All my canned responses seemed timid.

Yet now, years later, I know what I would share with him.

Think about these words from Paul in 1 Corinthians, chapter 15.

> For I delivered to you as of *first importance* what I also received, that Christ died for our sins in accordance with the scriptures.

"First importance" he says.

Read on:

> That he was buried, that he was raised on the third day in accordance with the scriptures, and that he appeared to Cephas, then to the twelve.[1]

There it is. Almost too simple. Jesus was killed, buried, and resurrected. Surprised? The part that matters is the cross. No more and no less.

The cross.

It rests on the time line of history like a compelling diamond. Its tragedy summons all sufferers. Its absurdity attracts all cynics. Its hope lures all searchers.

And according to Paul, the cross is what counts.

My, what a piece of wood! History has idolized it and despised it, gold-plated it and burned it, worn and trashed it. History has done everything to it but ignore it.

That's the one option that the cross does not offer.

No one can ignore it! You can't ignore a piece of lumber that suspends the greatest claim in history. A crucified carpenter claiming that he is God on earth? Divine? Eternal? The death-slayer?

No wonder Paul called it "the core of the gospel." Its bottom line is sobering: if the account is true, it is history's hinge. Period. If not, it is history's hoax.

That's why the cross is what matters. That's why if I had that cup of coffee to drink with Ian again I would tell him about it. I'd tell of the drama on that windy April day, the day when the kingdom of death was repossessed and hope took up the payments. I'd tell of Peter's tumble, Pilate's hesitancy, and John's loyalty. We'd read about the foggy garden of decision and the incandescent room of the resurrection. We'd discuss the final words uttered so deliberately by this self-sacrificing Messiah.

And finally, we'd look at the Messiah himself. A blue-collar Jew whose claim altered a world and whose promise has never been equaled.

No wonder they call him the Savior.

I'm wondering if I might not be addressing some readers who have the same question that Ian had. Oh, the cross is nothing new to you. You have seen it. You have worn it. You have thought about it. You have read about it. Maybe you have even prayed to it. But do you know it?

Any serious study of the Christian claim is, at its essence, a study of the cross. To accept or reject Christ without a careful examination of Calvary is like deciding on a car without looking at the engine. Being religious without knowing the cross is like owning a Mercedes with no motor. Pretty package, but where is your power?

Will you do me a favor? Get yourself some coffee, get comfortable, and give me an hour of your time. Take a good look at the cross with me. Let's examine this hour in history. Let's look at the witnesses. Let's listen to the voices. Let's watch the faces. And most of all, let's observe the one they call the Savior. And let's see if we can find the part that matters.

[1]1 Corinthians 15:3, 4 RSV, italics mine.

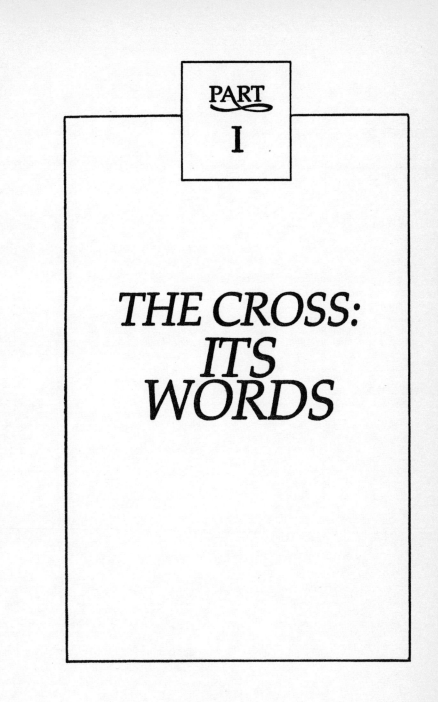

PART
I

THE CROSS: ITS WORDS

1

FINAL WORDS, FINAL ACTS

*I*n a recent trip to my hometown I took some time to go see a tree. "A live oak tree," my dad had called it (with the accent on "live"). It was nothing more than a sapling, so thin I could wrap my hand around it and touch my middle finger to my thumb. The West Texas wind scattered the fall leaves and caused me to zip up my coat. There is nothing colder than a prairie wind, especially in a cemetery.

"A special tree," I said to myself, "with a special job." I looked around. The cemetery was lined with elms but no oaks. The ground was dotted with tombstones but no trees. Just this one. A special tree for a special man.

About three years ago Daddy began noticing a steady weakening of his muscles. It began in his hands. He then felt it in his calves. Next his arms thinned a bit.

He mentioned his condition to my brother-in-law, who is a physician. My brother-in-law, alarmed, sent him to a specialist. The specialist conducted a lengthy battery of tests—blood, neurological, and muscular—and he reached his conclusion. Lou Gehrig's disease. A devastating crippler. No one knows the cause or the cure. The only sure thing about it is its cruelty and accuracy.

I looked down at the plot of ground that would someday entomb my father. Daddy always wanted to be buried under an oak tree so he bought this one. "Special order from the valley," he had boasted. "Had to get special permission from the city council to put it here." (That wasn't hard in this dusty oil field town where everybody knows everybody.)

The lump got tighter in my throat. A lesser man might have been angry. Another man might have given up. But Daddy didn't. He knew that his days were numbered so he began to get his house in order.

The tree was only one of the preparations he made. He improved the house for Mom by installing a sprinkler system and a garage door opener and by painting the trim. He got the will updated. He verified the insurance and retirement policies. He bought some stock to go toward his grandchildren's education. He planned his funeral. He bought cemetery plots for himself and Mom. He prepared his kids through words of assurance and letters of love. And last of all, he bought the tree. A live oak tree. (Pronounced with an accent on "live.")

Final acts. Final hours. Final words.

They reflect a life well lived. So do the last words of our Master. When on the edge of death, Jesus, too, got his house in order:

> A final prayer of forgiveness.
> A plea honored.
> A request of love.
> A question of suffering.
> A confession of humanity.
> A call of deliverance.
> A cry of completion.

Words of chance muttered by a desperate martyr? No. Words of intent, painted by the Divine Deliverer on the canvas of sacrifice.

Final words. Final acts. Each one is a window through which the cross can be better understood. Each one opens a treasury of promises. "So that is where you learned it," I said aloud as though speaking to my father. I smiled to myself and thought, "It's much easier to die like Jesus if you have lived like him for a lifetime."

The final hours are passing now. The gentle flame on his candle grows weaker and weaker. He lies in peace. His body dying, his spirit living. No longer can he get out of bed. He has chosen to live his last days at home. It won't be long. Death's windy draft will soon exhaust the flickering candle and it will be over.

I looked one last time at the slender oak. I touched it as if it had been hearing my thoughts. "Grow," I whispered. "Grow strong. Stand tall. Yours is a valued treasure."

As I drove home through the ragged oil field patchwork, I kept thinking about that tree. Though feeble, the decades will find it strong. Though slender, the years will add thickness and strength. Its last years will be its best. Just like my father's. Just like my Master's. "It is much easier to die like Jesus if you have lived like him for a lifetime."

"Grow, young tree." My eyes were misting. "Stand strong. Yours is a valued treasure."

He was awake when I got home. I leaned over his bed. "I checked on the tree," I told him. "It's growing."

He smiled.

2

WORDS THAT WOUND

"Father, forgive them" Luke 23:34.

T he dialogue that Friday morning was bitter.

From the onlookers, "Come down from the cross if you are the Son of God!"

From the religious leaders, "He saved others but he can't save himself."

From the soldiers, "If you are the king of the Jews, save yourself."

Bitter words. Acidic with sarcasm. Hateful. Irreverent. Wasn't it enough that he was being crucified? Wasn't it enough that he was being shamed as a criminal? Were the nails insufficient? Was the crown of thorns too soft? Had the flogging been too short?

For some, apparently so.

Peter, a writer not normally given to using many descriptive verbs, says that the passers-by "hurled" insults at the crucified Christ.[1] They didn't just yell or speak or scream. They "hurled" verbal stones. They had every intention of hurting and bruising. "We've broken the body, now let's break the spirit!" So they strung their bows with

23

self-righteousness and launched stinging arrows of pure poison.

Of all the scenes around the cross, this one angers me the most. What kind of people, I ask myself, would mock a dying man? Who would be so base as to pour the salt of scorn upon open wounds? How low and perverted to sneer at one who is laced with pain. Who would make fun of a person who is seated in an electric chair? Or who would point and laugh at a criminal who has a hangman's noose around his neck?

You can be sure that Satan and his demons were the cause of such filth.

And then the criminal on cross number two throws his punch.

"Aren't you the Christ? Save yourself and us!"

The words thrown that day were meant to wound. And there is nothing more painful than words meant to hurt. That's why James called the tongue a fire. Its burns are every bit as destructive and disastrous as those of a blowtorch.

But I'm not telling you anything new. No doubt you've had your share of words that wound. You've felt the sting of a well-aimed gibe. Maybe you're still feeling it. Someone you love or respect slams you to the floor with a slur or slip of the tongue. And there you lie, wounded and bleeding. Perhaps the words were intended to hurt you, perhaps not; but that doesn't matter. The wound is deep. The injuries are internal. Broken heart, wounded pride, bruised feelings.

Or maybe your wound is old. Though the arrow was extracted long ago, the arrowhead is still lodged . . . hidden under your skin. The old pain flares unpredictably and decisively, reminding you of harsh words yet unforgiven.

If you have suffered or are suffering because of someone else's words, you'll be glad to know that there is a balm for this laceration. Meditate on these words from 1 Peter 2:23.

> When they hurled their insults at him, he did not retaliate; when he suffered, he made no threats. Instead, he entrusted himself to him who judges justly.

Did you see what Jesus did not do? He did not retaliate. He did not bite back. He did not say, "I'll get you!" "Come on up here and say that to my face!" "Just wait until after the resurrection, buddy!" No, these statements were not found on Christ's lips.

Did you see what Jesus did do? He "entrusted himself to him who judges justly." Or said more simply, he left the judging to God. He did not take on the task of seeking revenge. He demanded no apology. He hired no bounty hunters and sent out no posse. He, to the astounding contrary, spoke on their defense. "Father, forgive them; for they do not know what they are doing."[2]

Yes, the dialogue that Friday morning was bitter. The verbal stones were meant to sting. How Jesus, with a body wracked with pain, eyes blinded by his own blood, and lungs yearning for air, could speak on behalf of some heartless thugs is beyond my comprehension. Never, never have I seen such love. If ever a person deserved a shot at revenge, Jesus did. But he didn't take it. Instead he died for them. How could he do it? I don't know. But I do know that all of a sudden my wounds seem very painless. My grudges and hard feelings are suddenly childish.

Sometimes I wonder if we don't see Christ's love as much in the people he tolerated as in the pain he endured.

Amazing Grace.

[1] 1 Peter 2:23
[2] Luke 23:34

3

VIGILANTE VENGEANCE

"They do not know what they are doing" Luke 23:34.

Thirty-seven years old. Thin, almost frail. Balding and bespectacled. An electronics buff. Law-abiding and timid. Certainly not a description you would give a vigilante. Certainly not the person you would cast to play Robin Hood or the Lone Ranger.

But that didn't bother the American public. When Bernhard Hugo Goetz blasted four would-be muggers in a New York subway, he instantly became a hero. A popular actress sent him a "love and kisses" telegram. "Thug-buster" T-shirts began to appear on the streets of New York City. A rock group wrote a song in his honor. People gave and raised money to go toward his defense. Radio talk shows were deluged with callers. "They won't let it go," said one radio host.

It's not hard to see why.

Bernhard Goetz was an American fantasy come true. He did what every citizen wants to do. He fought back. He "kicked the bully in the shins." He "punched the villain in the nose." He "clobbered evil over the head."

This unassuming hero embodied a nationwide, even worldwide anger: a passion for revenge.

The outpouring of support gives clear evidence. People are mad. People are angry. There is a pent-up, boiling rage that causes us to toast a man who fearlessly (or fearfully) says, "I ain't taking it no more!" and then comes out with a hot pistol in each hand.

We're tired. We're tired of being bullied, harassed, and intimidated. We're weary of the serial murderer, rapists, and hired assassins.

We're angry at someone, but we don't know who. We're scared of something, but we don't know what. We want to fight back, but we don't know how. And then, when a modern-day Wyatt Earp walks onto the scene, we applaud him. He is speaking for us! "That-a-way to go, Thug-Buster; that's the way to do it!"

Or is it? Is that really the way to do it? Let's think about our anger for just a minute.

Anger. It's a peculiar yet predictable emotion. It begins as a drop of water. An irritant. A frustration. Nothing big, just an aggravation. Someone gets your parking place. Someone pulls in front of you on the freeway. A waitress is slow and you are in a hurry. The toast burns. Drops of water. Drip. Drip. Drip. Drip.

Yet, get enough of these seemingly innocent drops of anger and before long you've got a bucket full of rage. Walking revenge. Blind bitterness. Unharnessed hatred. We trust no one and bare our teeth at anyone who gets near. We become walking time bombs that, given just the right tension and fear, could explode like Mr. Goetz.

Now, is that any way to live? What good has hatred ever brought? What hope has anger ever created? What problems have ever been resolved by revenge?

No one can blame the American public for applauding the man who fought back. Yet, as the glamor fades on such acts, reality makes us ask the questions: What good was done? Is that really the way to reduce the crime rate? Are subways forever safer? Are the streets now free of fear? No. Anger doesn't do that. Anger only feeds a primitive lust for revenge that feeds our anger that feeds our revenge that feeds our anger—you get the picture. Vigilantes are not the answer.

Yet, what do we do? We can't deny that our anger exists. How do we harness it? A good option is found in Luke 23:34. Here, Jesus speaks about the mob that killed him. " 'Father forgive them, for they do not know what they are doing.' "

Have you ever wondered how Jesus kept from retaliating? Have you ever asked how he kept his control? Here's the answer. It's the second part of his statement: "for they do not know what they are doing." Look carefully. It's as if Jesus considered this bloodthirsty, death-hungry crowd not as murderers, but as victims. It's as if he saw in their faces not hatred but confusion. It's as if he regarded them not as a militant mob but, as he put it, as "sheep without a shepherd."

"They don't know what they are doing."

And when you think about it, they didn't. They hadn't the faintest idea what they were doing. They were a stir-crazy mob, mad at something they couldn't see so they took it out on, of all people, God. But they didn't know what they were doing.

And for the most part, neither do we. We are still, as much as we hate to admit it, shepherdless sheep. All we know is that we were born out of one eternity and are frighteningly close to another. We play tag with the fuzzy realities of death and pain. We can't answer our own questions about love and hurt. We can't solve the riddle of aging. We don't know how to heal our own bodies or get along with our own mates. We can't keep ourselves out of war. We can't even keep ourselves fed.

Paul spoke for humanity when he confessed, "I do not know what I am doing."[1]

Now, I know that doesn't justify anything. That doesn't justify hit-and-run drivers or kiddie-porn peddlers or heroin dealers. But it does help explain why they do the miserable things they do.

My point is this: Uncontrolled anger won't better our world, but sympathetic understanding will. Once we see the world and ourselves for what we are, we can help. Once we understand ourselves we begin to operate not from a posture of anger but of compassion and concern. We look at the world not with bitter frowns but with extended hands. We realize that the lights are out and a lot of people are stumbling in the darkness. So we light candles.

As Michelangelo said, "we criticize by creating." Instead of fighting back we help out. We go to the ghettos. We teach in the schools. We build hospitals and help orphans . . . and we put away our guns.

"They do not know what they are doing."

There is something about understanding the world that makes us want to save it, even to die for it. Anger? Anger never did anyone any good. Understanding? Well, the results are not as quick as the vigilante's bullet, but they are certainly much more constructive.

[1]Romans 7:15, author's paraphrase.

4

THE TALE OF THE CRUCIFIED CROOK

"I tell you the truth, today you will be with me in paradise" Luke 23:43.

The only thing more outlandish than the request was that it was granted. Just trying to picture the scene is enough to short-circuit the most fanciful of imaginations; a flatnosed ex-con asking God's son for eternal life? But trying to imagine the appeal being honored, well, that steps beyond the realm of reality and enters absurdity.

But as absurd as it may appear, that's exactly what happened. He who deserved hell got heaven, and we are left with a puzzling riddle. What, for goodness' sake, was Jesus trying to teach us? What was he trying to prove by pardoning this strong-arm, who in all probability had never said grace, much less done anything to deserve it?

Well, I've got a theory. But to explain it, I've got to tell you a tale that you may not believe.

It seems a couple of prowlers broke into a department store in a large city. They successfully entered the store, stayed long enough to do what they came to do, and escaped unnoticed. What is unusual about the story is what these fellows did. They took nothing. Absolutely nothing. No merchandise was stolen. No items were removed. But what they did do was ridiculous.

Instead of stealing anything, they changed the cost of everything. Price tags were swapped. Values were exchanged. These clever pranksters took the tag off a $395.00 camera and stuck it on a $5.00 box of stationery. The $5.95 sticker on a paperback book was removed and placed on an outboard motor. They repriced everything in the store!

Crazy? You bet. But the craziest part of this story took place the next morning. (You are not going to believe this.) The store opened as usual. Employees went to work. Customers began to shop. The place functioned as normal for four hours before anyone noticed what had happened.

Four hours! Some people got some great bargains. Others got fleeced. For four solid hours no one noticed that all the values had been swapped.

Hard to believe? It shouldn't be—we see the same thing happening every day. We are deluged by a distorted value system. We see the most valuable things in our lives peddled for pennies and we see the cheapest smut go for millions.

The examples are abundant and besetting. Here are a few that I've encountered in the last week.

The salesman who defended his illegal practices by saying, "Let's not confuse business with ethics."

The military men who sold top-secret information (as well as their integrity) for $6,000.

The cabinet member of a large nation who was caught illegally dealing in semi-precious stones. His cabinet position? Minister of *Justice*.

The father who confessed to the murder of his

twelve-year-old daughter. The reason he killed her? She refused to go to bed with him.

Why do we do what we do? Why do we take blatantly black-and-white and paint it gray? Why are priceless mores trashed while senseless standards are obeyed? What causes us to elevate the body and degrade the soul? What causes us to pamper the skin while we pollute the heart?

Our values are messed up. Someone broke into the store and exchanged all the price tags. Thrills are going for top dollar and the value of human beings is at an all-time low.

One doesn't have to be a philosopher to determine what caused such a sag in the market. It all began when someone convinced us that the human race is headed nowhere. That man has no *destiny*. That we are in a cycle. That there is no reason or rhyme to this absurd existence. Somewhere we got the idea that we are meaninglessly trapped on a puny mudheap that has no destination. The earth is just a spinning mausoleum and the universe is purposeless. The creation was incidental and humanity has no direction.

Pretty gloomy, huh?

The second verse is even worse. If man has no destiny, then he has no *duty*. No obligation, no responsibility. If man has no destiny, then he has no guidelines or goals. If man has no destiny, then who is to say what is right or wrong? Who is to say that a husband can't leave his wife and family? Who is to say you can't abort a fetus? What is wrong with shacking up? Who says I can't step on someone's neck to get to the top? It's your value system against mine. No absolutes. No principles. No ethics. No standards. Life is reduced to weekends, paychecks, and quick thrills. The bottom line is disaster.

"The existentialist," writes existentialist Jean-Paul Sartre, "finds it extremely embarrassing that God does not exist, for there disappears with him all possibility of finding values in an intelligible heaven. . . . Everything is indeed permitted if God does not exist, and man is in consequence forlorn, for he cannot find anything to depend on within or without himself."[1]

If man has no duty or destiny, the next logical step is that man has no *value*. If man has no future, he isn't worth much. He is worth, in fact, about as much as a tree or a rock. No difference. There is no reason to be here, therefore, there is no value.

And you've seen the results of this. Our system goes haywire. We feel useless and worthless. We freak out. We play games. We create false value systems. We say that you are valuable if you are pretty. We say that you are valuable if you can produce. We say that you are valuable if you can slam-dunk a basketball or snag a pop fly. You are valuable if your name has a "Dr." in front of it or Ph.D. on the end of it. You are valuable if you have a six-figure salary and drive a foreign car.

Value is now measured by two criteria, appearance and performance.

Pretty tough system, isn't it? Where does that leave the retarded? Or the ugly or uneducated? Where does that place the aged or the handicapped? What hope does that offer the unborn child? Not much. Not much at all. We become nameless numbers on mislaid lists.

Now please understand, this is man's value system. It is not God's. His plan is much brighter. God, with eyes twinkling, steps up to the philosopher's blackboard, erases the never-ending, ever-repeating circle of history and replaces it with a line; a hopefilled, promising, slender line. And, looking over his shoulder to see if the class is watching, he draws an arrow on the end.

In God's book man is heading somewhere. He has an amazing destiny. We are being prepared to walk down the church aisle and become the bride of Jesus. We are going to live with him. Share the throne with him. Reign with him. We count. We are valuable. And what's more, our worth is built in! Our value is inborn.

You see, if there was anything that Jesus wanted everyone to understand it was this: A person is worth something simply because he is a person. That is why he treated people like he did. Think about it. The girl caught making undercover thunder with someone she shouldn't—he forgave her. The untouchable leper who asked for cleansing—he touched him. And the blind welfare case that cluttered the roadside—he honored him. And the worn-out old windbag addicted to self-pity near the pool of Siloam—he healed him!

And don't forget the classic case study on the value of a person by Luke. It is called "The Tale of the Crucified Crook."

If anyone was ever worthless, this one was. If any man ever deserved dying, this man probably did. If any fellow was ever a loser, this fellow was at the top of the list.

Perhaps that is why Jesus chose him to show us what he thinks of the human race.

Maybe this criminal had heard the Messiah speak. Maybe he had seen him love the lowly. Maybe he had watched him dine with the punks, pickpockets, and potmouths on the streets. Or maybe not. Maybe the only thing he knew about this Messiah was what he now saw: a beaten, slashed, nail-suspended preacher. His face crimson with blood, his bones peeking through torn flesh, his lungs gasping for air.

Something, though, told him he had never been in better company. And somehow he realized that even though all he had was prayer, he had finally met the One to whom he should pray.

"Any chance that you could put in a good word for me?" (Loose translation.)

"Consider it done."

Now why did Jesus do that? What in the world did he have to gain by promising this desperado a place of honor at the banquet table? What in the world could this chiseling quisling ever offer in return? I mean, the Samaritan woman I can understand. She could go back and tell the tale. And Zacchaeus had some money that he could give. But this guy? What is he going to do? Nothing!

That's the point. Listen closely. Jesus' love does not depend upon what we do for him. Not at all. In the eyes of the King, you have value simply because you are. You don't have to look nice or perform well. Your value is inborn.

Period.

Think about that for just a minute. You are valuable just because you exist. Not because of what you do or what you have done, but simply because you are. Remember that. Remember that the next time you are left bobbing in the wake of someone's steamboat ambition. Remember that the next time some trickster tries to hang a bargain basement price tag on your self-worth. The next time someone tries to pass you off as a cheap buy, just think about the way Jesus honors you . . . and smile.

I do. I smile because I know I don't deserve love like that. None of us do. When you get right down to it, any contribution that any of us make is pretty puny. All of us—even the purest of us—deserve heaven about as much as that crook did. All of us are signing on Jesus' credit card, not ours.

And it also makes me smile to think that there is a grinning ex-con walking the golden streets who knows more about grace than a thousand theologians. No one else would have given him a prayer. But in the end that is all that he had. And in the end, that is all it took.

No wonder they call him the Savior.

[1]Walter Kaufman, ed., *Existentialism from Dostoyevsky to Sartre*, New York, Meridian Books, 1956, pp. 294-295).

5

LEAVING IS LOVING

"Woman, behold your son" John 19:26 RSV

The gospel is full of rhetorical challenges that test our faith and buck against human nature.

"It is more blessed to give than to receive."[1]

"For whoever wants to save his life will lose it, but whoever loses his life for me will save it."[2]

"Only in his home town and in his own house is a prophet without honor."[3]

But no statement is as confusing or frightening as the one in Matthew 19:29. "And everyone who has left houses or brothers or sisters or father or mother or children or fields for my sake will receive a hundred times as much and will inherit eternal life."

The part about leaving land and fields I can understand. It is the other part that causes me to cringe. It's the part about leaving mom and dad, saying goodbye to brothers and sisters, placing a farewell kiss on a son or daughter. It is easy to parallel discipleship with poverty or public disgrace, but leaving my family? Why do I have to be willing to leave those I love? Can sacrifice get any more sacrificial than that?

"Woman, behold your son."

Mary is older now. The hair at her temples is gray. Wrinkles have replaced her youthful skin. Her hands are calloused. She has raised a houseful of children. And now she beholds the crucifixion of her firstborn.

One wonders what memories she conjures up as she witnesses his torture. The long ride to Bethlehem, perhaps. A baby's bed made from cow's hay. Fugitives in Egypt. At home in Nazareth. Panic in Jerusalem. "I thought he was with you!" Carpentry lessons. Dinner table laughter.

And then the morning Jesus came in from the shop early, his eyes firmer, his voice more direct. He had heard the news. "John is preaching in the desert." Her son took off his nail apron, dusted off his hands, and with one last look said goodbye to his mother. They both knew it would never be the same again. In that last look they shared a secret, the full extent of which was too painful to say aloud.

Mary learned that day the heartache that comes from saying goodbye. From then on she was to love her son from a distance; on the edge of the crowd, outside of a packed house, on the shore of the sea. Maybe she was even there when the enigmatic promise was made, "Anyone who has left . . . mother . . . for my sake."

Mary wasn't the first one to be called to say goodbye to loved ones for sake of the kingdom. Joseph was called to be an orphan in Egypt. Jonah was called to be a foreigner in Nineveh. Hannah sent her firstborn son away to serve in the temple. Daniel was sent from Jerusalem to Babylon. Nehemiah was sent from Susa to Jerusalem. Abraham was sent to sacrifice his own son. Paul had to say goodbye to his heritage. The Bible is bound together with goodbye trails and stained with farewell tears.

In fact, it seems that *goodbye* is a word all too prevalent in the Christian's vocabulary. Missionaries know it well. Those who send them know it, too. The doctor who leaves the city to work in the jungle hospital has said it. So has the Bible translator who lives far from home. Those who feed the hungry, those who teach the lost, those who help the poor all know the word goodbye.

Airports. Luggage. Embraces. Taillights. "Wave to grandma." Tears. Bus terminals. Ship docks. "Goodbye Daddy." Tight throats. Ticket counters. Misty eyes. "Write me!"

Question: What kind of God would put people through such agony? What kind of God would give you families and then ask you to leave them? What kind of God would give you friends and then ask you to say goodbye?

Answer: A God who knows that the deepest love is built not on passion and romance but on a common mission and sacrifice.

Answer: A God who knows that we are only pilgrims and that eternity is so close that any "Goodbye" is in reality a "See you tomorrow."

Answer: A God who did it himself.

"Woman, behold your son."

John fastened his arm around Mary a little tighter. Jesus was asking him to be the son that a mother needs and that in some ways he never was.

Jesus looked at Mary. His ache was from a pain far greater than that of the nails and thorns. In their silent glance they again shared a secret. And he said goodbye.

[1]Acts 20:35
[2]Luke 9:24
[3]Matthew 13:57

6

THE CRY OF LONELINESS

"My God, my God, why have you forsaken me?"
Matthew 27:46

For those of us who endured it, the summer of 1980 in Miami was nothing to smile about. The Florida heat scorched the city during the day and baked it at night. Riots, lootings, and racial tension threatened to snap the frayed emotions of the people. Everything soared: unemployment, inflation, the crime rate, and especially the thermometer. Somewhere in the midst of it all, a Miami Herald reporter captured a story that left the entire Gold Coast breathless. It was the story of Judith Bucknell. Attractive, young, successful, and dead.

Judith Bucknell was homicide number one hundred and six that year. She was killed on a steamy June 9th evening. Age: 38. Weight: 109 pounds. Stabbed seven times. Strangled.

She kept a diary. Had she not kept this diary perhaps the memory of her would have been buried with her body. But the diary exists; a painful epitaph to a lonely life. The correspondent made this comment about her writings:

In her diaries, Judy created a character and a voice. The character is herself, wistful, struggling, weary; the voice is yearning. Judith Bucknell has failed to connect; age 38, many lovers, much love offered, none returned.[1]

Her struggles weren't unusual. She worried about getting old, getting fat, getting married, getting pregnant, and getting by. She lived in stylish Coconut Grove (Coconut Grove is where you live if you are lonely but act happy).

Judy was the paragon of the confused human being. Half of her life was fantasy, half was nightmare. Successful as a secretary, but a loser at love. Her diary was replete with entries such as the following.

Where are the men with the flowers and champagne and music? Where are the men who call and ask for a genuine, actual date? Where are the men who would like to share more than my bed, my booze, my food. . . . I would like to have in my life, once before I pass through my life, the kind of sexual relationship which is part of a loving relationship.[2]

She never did.

Judy was not a prostitute. She was not on drugs or on welfare. She never went to jail. She was not a social outcast. She was respectable. She jogged. She hosted parties. She wore designer clothes and had an apartment that overlooked the bay. And she was very lonely. "I see people together and I'm so jealous I want to throw up. What about me! What about me!" Though surrounded by people, she was on an island. Though she had many acquaintances, she had few friends. Though she had many lovers (fifty-nine in fifty-six months), she had little love.

"Who is going to love Judy Bucknell?" the diary continues. "I feel so old. Unloved. Unwanted. Abandoned. Used up. I want to cry and sleep forever."[3]

A clear message came from her aching words. Though her body died on June 9th from the wounds of a knife, her heart had died long before . . . from loneliness.

"I'm alone," she wrote, "and I want to share something with somebody."[4]

Loneliness.

It's a cry. A moan, a wail. It's a gasp whose origin is the recesses of our souls.

Can you hear it? The abandoned child. The divorcée. The quiet home. The empty mailbox. The long days. The longer nights. A one-night stand. A forgotten birthday. A silent phone.

Cries of loneliness. Listen again. Tune out the traffic and turn down the TV. The cry is there. Our cities are full of Judy Bucknells. You can hear their cries. You can hear them in the convalescent home among the sighs and the shuffling feet. You can hear them in the prisons among the moans of shame and the calls for mercy. You can hear them if you walk the manicured streets of suburban America, among the aborted ambitions and aging homecoming queens. Listen for it in the halls of our high schools where peer pressure weeds out the "have-nots" from the "haves."

This moan in a minor key knows all spectrums of society. From the top to the bottom. From the failures to the famous. From the poor to the rich. From the married to the single. Judy Bucknell was not alone.

Many of you have been spared this cruel cry. Oh, you have been homesick or upset a time or two. But despair? Far from it. Suicide? Of course not. Be thankful that it hasn't knocked on your door. Pray that it never will. If you have yet to fight this battle, you are welcome to read on if you wish, but I'm really writing to someone else.

I am writing to those who know this cry firsthand. I'm writing to those of you whose days are bookended with broken hearts and long evenings. I'm writing to those of you who can find a lonely person simply by looking in the mirror.

For you, loneliness is a way of life. The sleepless nights. The lonely bed. The distrust. The fear of tomorrow. The unending hurt.

When did it begin? In your childhood? At the divorce? At retirement? At the cemetery? When the kids left home?

Maybe you, like Judy Bucknell, have fooled everyone. No one knows that you are lonely. On the outside you are packaged perfectly. Your smile is quick. Your job is stable. Your clothes are sharp. Your waist is thin. Your calendar is full. Your walk brisk. Your talk impressive. But when you look in the mirror, you fool no one. When you are alone, the duplicity ceases and the pain surfaces.

Or maybe you don't try to hide it. Maybe you have always been outside the circle looking in, and everyone knows it. Your conversation is a bit awkward. Your companionship is seldom requested. Your clothes are dull. Your looks are common. Ziggy is your hero and Charlie Brown is your mentor.

Am I striking a chord? If I am, if you have nodded or sighed in understanding, I have an important message for you.

The most gut-wrenching cry of loneliness in history came not from a prisoner or a widow or a patient. It came from a hill, from a cross, from a Messiah.

"My God, my God!" he screamed, "Why did you abandon me!"[5]

Never have words carried so much hurt. Never has one being been so lonely.

The crowd quietens as the priest receives the goat; the pure, unspotted goat. In somber ceremony he places his hands on the young animal. As the people witness, the priest makes his proclamation. "The sins of the people be upon you." The innocent animal receives the sins of the Israelites. All the lusting, adultery, and cheating are transferred from the sinners to this goat, to this scapegoat.

He is then carried to the edge of the wilderness and released. Banished. Sin must be purged, so the scapegoat is abandoned. "Run, goat! Run!"

The people are relieved.

Yahweh is appeased.

The sinbearer is alone.[6]

And now on Skull's hill, the sinbearer is again alone. Every lie ever told, every object ever coveted, every promise ever broken is on his shoulders. He is sin.

God turns away. "Run, goat! Run!"

The despair is darker than the sky. The two who have been one are now two. Jesus, who had been with God for eternity, is now alone. The Christ, who was an expression of God, is abandoned. The Trinity is dismantled. The Godhead is disjointed. The unity is dissolved.

It is more than Jesus can take. He withstood the beatings and remained strong at the mock trials. He watched in silence as those he loved ran away. He did not retaliate when the insults were hurled nor did he scream when the nails pierced his wrists.

But when God turned his head, that was more than he could handle.

"My God!" The wail rises from parched lips. The holy heart is broken. The sinbearer screams as he wanders in the eternal wasteland. Out of the silent sky come the words screamed by all who walk in the desert of loneliness. "Why? Why did you abandon me?"

I can't understand it. I honestly cannot. Why did Jesus do it? Oh, I know, I know. I have heard the official answers. "To gratify the old law." "To fulfill prophecy." And these answers are right. They are. But there is something more here. Something very compassionate. Something yearning. Something personal.

What is it?

I may be wrong, but I keep thinking of the diary. "I feel abandoned," she wrote. "Who is going to love Judith Bucknell?" And I keep thinking of the parents of the dead child. Or the friend at the hospital bedside. Or the elderly in the nursing home. Or the orphans. Or the cancer ward.

I keep thinking of all the people who cast despairing eyes toward the dark heavens and cry "Why?"

And I imagine him. I imagine him listening. I picture his eyes misting and a pierced hand brushing away a tear. And although he may offer no answer, although he may solve no dilemma, although the question may freeze painfully in mid-air, he who also was once alone, understands.

[1]Madeleine Blais, "Who's Going to Love Judy Bucknell?" (Part 1), Tropic Magazine, *The Miami Herald*, 12 October 1980.

[2]Ibid.

[3]Ibid.

[4]Ibid.

[5]Matthew 27:46 Good News

[6]Leviticus 16:22 (author's paraphrase)

7

I THIRST

Later, knowing that all was now completed, and so that
the Scripture would be fulfilled, Jesus said, "I am thirsty"
John 19:28.

I.

I' m tired," he sighed. So he stopped. "You go
on and get the food. I'll rest right here." He was
tired. Bone-tired. His feet were hurting. His face was hot.
The noon sun was sizzling. He wanted to rest. So he
stopped at the well, waved on his disciples, stretched a bit,
and sat down. But before he could close his eyes, here
came a Samaritan woman. She was alone. Maybe it was the
bags under her eyes or the way she stooped that made him
forget how weary he was. "How strange that she should
be here at midday."

II.

"I'm sleepy." He stretched. He yawned. It had
been a long day. The crowd had been large, so large that
preaching on the beach had proved to be an occupational
hazard, so he had taught from the bow of a fishing boat.
And now night had fallen and Jesus was sleepy. "If you
guys don't mind, I'm going to catch a few winks." So he
did. On a cloud-covered night on the Sea of Galilee, God

went to sleep. Someone rustled him up a pillow and he went to the boat's driest point and sacked out. So deep was his sleep, the thunder did not wake him. Nor did the tossing of the boat. Nor did the salty spray of the storm-blown waves. Only the screams of some breathless disciples could penetrate his slumber.

III.

"I'm angry." He didn't have to say it; you could see it in his eyes. Face red. Blood vessels bulging. Fists clenched. "I ain't taking this no more!" And what was a temple became a one-sided barroom brawl. What was a normal day at the market became a one-man riot. And what was a smile on the face of the Son of God became a scowl. "Get out of here!" The only thing that flew higher than the tables were the doves flapping their way to freedom. An angry Messiah made his point: don't go making money off religion, or God will make hay of you!

We are indebted to Matthew, Mark, Luke, and John for choosing to include these tidbits of humanity. They didn't have to, you know. But they did—and at just the right times.

Just as his divinity is becoming unapproachable, just when his holiness is becoming untouchable, just when his perfection becomes inimitable, the phone rings and a voice whispers, "He was human. Don't forget. He had flesh."

Just at the right time we are reminded that the one to whom we pray knows our feelings. He knows temptation. He has felt discouraged. He has been hungry and sleepy and tired. He knows what we feel like when the alarm clock goes off. He knows what we feel like when our children want different things at the same time. He nods in understanding when we pray in anger. He is touched when we tell him there is more to do than can ever be done. He smiles when we confess our weariness.

But we are most indebted to John for choosing to include verse 28 of chapter 19. It reads simply:

"I'm thirsty."

That's not THE CHRIST that's thirsty. That's the carpenter. And those are words of humanity in the midst of divinity.

This phrase messes up your sermon outline. The other six statements are more "in character." They are cries we would expect: forgiving sinners, promising paradise, caring for his mother, even the cry "My God, My God, why have you forsaken me" is one of power.

But, "I thirst?"

Just when we had it all figured out. Just when the cross was all packaged and defined. Just when the manuscript was finished. Just when we had invented all those nice clean "ation" words like sanctification, justification, propitiation, and purification. Just when we put our big golden cross on our big golden steeple, he reminds us that "the Word became flesh."

He wants us to remember that he, too, was human. He wants us to know that he, too, knew the drone of the humdrum and the weariness that comes with long days. He wants us to remember that our trailblazer didn't wear bulletproof vests or rubber gloves or an impenetrable suit of armor. No, he pioneered our salvation through the world that you and I face daily.

He is the King of Kings, the Lord of Lords, and the Word of Life. More than ever he is the Morning Star, the Horn of Salvation, and the Prince of Peace.

But there are some hours when we are restored by remembering that God became flesh and dwelt among us. Our Master knew what it meant to be a crucified carpenter who got thirsty.

8

CREATIVE COMPASSION

"It is finished" John 19:30.

"In the beginning God *created* the heavens and the earth."[1] That's what it says. "God *created* the heavens and the earth." It doesn't say, "God *made* the heavens and the earth." Nor does it say that he "xeroxed" the heavens and the earth. Or "built" or "developed" or "mass-produced." No, the word is "created."

And that one word says a lot. Creating is something far different than constructing. The difference is pretty obvious. Constructing something engages only the hands while creating something engages the heart and the soul.

You've probably noticed this in your own life. Think about something you've created. A painting perhaps. Or a song. Those lines of poetry you never showed to anyone. Or even the doghouse in the backyard.

How do you feel toward that creation? Good? I hope so. Proud? Even protective? You should. Part of you lives in that project. When you create something you are putting yourself into it. It's far greater than an ordinary assignment or task; it's an expression of you!

Now, imagine God's creativity. Of all we don't know about the creation, there is one thing we do know—he did it with a smile. He must've had a blast. Painting the stripes on the zebra, hanging the stars in the sky, putting the gold in the sunset. What creativity! Stretching the neck of the giraffe, putting the flutter in the mockingbird's wings, planting the giggle in the hyena.

What a time he had. Like a whistling carpenter in his workshop, he loved every bit of it. He poured himself into the work. So intent was his creativity that he took a day off at the end of the week just to rest.

And then, as a finale to a brilliant performance, he made man. With his typical creative flair, he began with a useless mound of dirt and ended up with an invaluable species called a human. A human who had the unique honor to bear the stamp, "In His Image."

At this point in the story one would be tempted to jump and clap. "Bravo!" "Encore!" "Unmatchable!" "Beautiful!"

But the applause would be premature. The Divine Artist has yet to unveil his greatest creation.

As the story unfolds, a devil of a snake feeds man a line and an apple, and gullible Adam swallows them both. This one act of rebellion sets in motion a dramatic and erratic courtship between God and man. Though the characters and scenes change, the scenario repeats itself endlessly. God, still the compassionate Creator, woos his creation. Man, the creation, alternately reaches out in repentance and runs in rebellion.

It is within this simple script that God's creativity flourishes. If you thought he was imaginative with the sea and the stars, just wait until you read what he does to get his creation to listen to him!

For example:

  A ninety-year-old woman gets pregnant.
  A woman turns to salt.
  A flood blankets the earth.
  A bush burns (but doesn't burn up!).
  The Red Sea splits in two.
  The walls of Jericho fall.
  The sky rains fire.
  A donkey speaks.

Talk about special effects! But these acts, be they ever ingenious, still couldn't compare with what was to come.

Nearing the climax of the story, God, motivated by love and directed by divinity, surprised everyone. He became a man. In an untouchable mystery, he disguised himself as a carpenter and lived in a dusty Judaean village. Determined to prove his love for his creation, he walked incognito through his own world. His calloused hands touched wounds and his compassionate words touched hearts. He became one of us.

Have you ever seen such determination? Have you ever witnessed such a desire to communicate? If one thing didn't work, he'd try another. If one approach failed, he'd try a new one. His mind never stopped. "In the past God spoke . . . at *many* times and in *various* ways," writes the author of Hebrews, "but in these last days he has spoken to us by his Son."[2]

But as beautiful as this act of incarnation was, it was not the zenith. Like a master painter God reserved his masterpiece until the end. All the earlier acts of love had been leading to this one. The angels hushed and the heavens paused to witness the finale. God unveils the canvas and the ultimate act of creative compassion is revealed.

God on a cross.

The Creator being sacrificed for the creation. God convincing man once and for all that forgiveness still follows failure.

I wonder if, while on the cross, the Creator allowed his thoughts to wander back to the beginning. One wonders if he allowed the myriad of faces and acts to parade in his memory. Did he reminisce about the creation of the sky and sea? Did he relive the conversations with Abraham and Moses? Did he remember the plagues and the promises, the wilderness and the wanderings? We don't know.

We do know, however, what he said.

"It is finished."

The mission was finished. All that the master painter needed to do was done and was done in splendor. His creation could now come home.

"It is finished!" he cried.

And the great Creator went home.

(He's not resting, though. Word has it that his tireless hands are preparing a city so glorious that even the angels get goosebumps upon seeing it. Considering what he has done so far, that is one creation I plan to see.)

[1]Genesis 1:1, italics mine.
[2]Hebrews 1:1-2, italics mine.

9

IT IS FINISHED

"It is finished" John 19:30.

Several years ago, Paul Simon and Art Garfunkel enchanted us all with the song of a poor boy who went to New York on a dream and fell victim to the harsh life of the city. Penniless, with only strangers as friends, he spent his days "laying low, seeking out the poorer quarters where the ragged people go, looking for the places only they would know."[1]

It's easy to picture this young lad, dirty face and worn clothes, looking for work and finding none. He trudges the sidewalks and battles the cold, and dreams of going somewhere "where the New York City winters aren't bleeding me, leading me home."

He entertains thoughts of quitting. Going home. Giving up—something he never thought he would do.

But just when he picks up the towel to throw it into the ring he encounters a boxer. Remember these words?

> In the clearing stands a boxer and a
> fighter by his trade, and he carries a re-
> minder of every blow that laid him

down or cut him till he cried out in his anger and his shame—'I am leaving, I am leaving!' but the fighter still remains.[2]

"The fighter still remains." There is something magnetic in that phrase. It rings with a trueness.

Those who can remain like the boxer are a rare breed. I don't necessarily mean win, I just mean remain. Hang in there. Finish. Stick to it until it is done. But unfortunately, very few of us do that. Our human tendency is to quit too soon. Our human tendency is to stop before we cross the finish line.

Our inability to finish what we start is seen in the smallest of things:

> A partly mowed lawn.
> A half-read book.
> Letters begun but never completed.
> An abandoned diet.
> A car up on blocks.

Or, it shows up in life's most painful areas:

> An abandoned child.
> A cold faith.
> A job hopper.
> A wrecked marriage.
> An unevangelized world.

Am I touching some painful sores? Any chance I'm addressing someone who is considering giving up? If I am, I want to encourage you to remain. I want to encourage you to remember Jesus' determination on the cross.

Jesus didn't quit. But don't think for one minute that he wasn't tempted to. Watch him wince as he hears his apostles backbite and quarrel. Look at him weep as he sits at Lazarus's tomb or hear him wail as he claws the ground of Gethsemane.

Did he ever want to quit? You bet.

That's why his words are so splendid.

"It is finished."

Stop and listen. Can you imagine the cry from the cross? The sky is dark. The other two victims are moaning. The jeering mouths are silent. Perhaps there is thunder. Perhaps there is weeping. Perhaps there is silence. Then Jesus draws in a deep breath, pushes his feet down on that Roman nail, and cries, "It is finished!"

What was finished?

The history-long plan of redeeming man was finished. The message of God to man was finished. The works done by Jesus as a man on earth were finished. The task of selecting and training ambassadors was finished. The job was finished. The song had been sung. The blood had been poured. The sacrifice had been made. The sting of death had been removed. It was over.

A cry of defeat? Hardly. Had his hands not been fastened down I dare say that a triumphant fist would have punched the dark sky. No, this is no cry of despair. It is a cry of completion. A cry of victory. A cry of fulfillment. Yes, even a cry of relief.

The fighter remained. And thank God that he did. Thank God that he endured.

Are you close to quitting? Please don't do it. Are you discouraged as a parent? Hang in there. Are you weary with doing good? Do just a little more. Are you pessimistic about your job? Roll up your sleeves and go at it again. No communication in your marriage? Give it one more shot. Can't resist temptation? Accept God's forgiveness and go one more round. Is your day framed with sorrow and disappointment? Are your tomorrows turning into nevers? Is hope a forgotten word?

Remember, a finisher is not one with no wounds or weariness. Quite to the contrary, he, like the boxer, is scarred and bloody. Mother Teresa is credited with saying, "God didn't call us to be successful, just faithful." The fighter, like our Master, is pierced and full of pain. He, like Paul, may even be bound and beaten. But he remains.

The Land of Promise, says Jesus, awaits those who endure.[3] It is not just for those who make the victory laps or drink champagne. No sir. The Land of Promise is for those who simply remain to the end.

Let's endure.

Listen to this chorus of verses designed to give us staying power:

> Consider it pure joy, my brothers, whenever you face trials of many kinds, because you know that the testing of your faith develops perseverance.[4]

> Therefore lift your drooping hands and strengthen your weak knees, and make straight paths for your feet so that what is lame may not be put out of joint but rather be healed.[5]

> Let us not become weary in doing good, for at the proper time we will reap a harvest if we do not give up.[6]

> I have fought the good fight, I have finished the race, I have kept the faith.

Now there is in store for me the crown of righteousness, which the Lord, the righteous Judge, will award to me on that day—and not only to me, but also to all who have longed for his appearing.[7]

Blessed is the man who perseveres under trial, because when he has stood the test, he will receive the crown of life that God has promised to those who love him.[8]

Thank you, Paul Simon. Thank you, apostle Paul. Thank you, apostle James. But most of all, thank you, Lord Jesus, for teaching us to remain, to endure, and in the end, to finish.

[1]"The Boxer" by Paul Simon © 1968.
[2]Ibid.
[3]Matthew 10:22.
[4]James 1:2-3.
[5]Hebrews 12:12-13 RSV.
[6]Galatians 6:9.
[7]2 Timothy 4:7-9.
[8]James 1:12.

10

TAKE ME HOME

"Father, into your hands I commit my spirit"
Luke 23:46.

Were it a war—this would be the aftermath.
Were it a symphony—this would be the second be-
    tween the final note and the
    first applause.
Were it a journey—this would be the sight of home.
Were it a storm—this would be the sun, piercing the
    clouds.
But it wasn't. It was a Messiah. And this was a sigh of joy.

"Father!" (The voice is hoarse.)
The voice that called forth the dead,
the voice that taught the willing,
the voice that screamed at God,
  now says, "Father!"
  "Father."

 The two are again one.
 The abandoned is now found.
 The schism is now bridged.

"Father." He smiles weakly. "It's over."
  Satan's vultures have been scattered.
  Hell's demons have been jailed.
  Death has been damned.
  The sun is out,
    The Son is out.

It's over.
An angel sighs. A star wipes away a tear.

"Take me home."
Yes, take him home.
Take this prince to his king.
Take this son to his father.
Take this pilgrim to his home.
      (He deserves a rest.)

"Take me home."
Come ten thousand angels! Come and take this wounded
troubador to
the cradle of his Father's arms!

Farewell manger's infant.
Bless You holy ambassador.
Go Home death slayer.
Rest well sweet soldier.

      The battle is over.

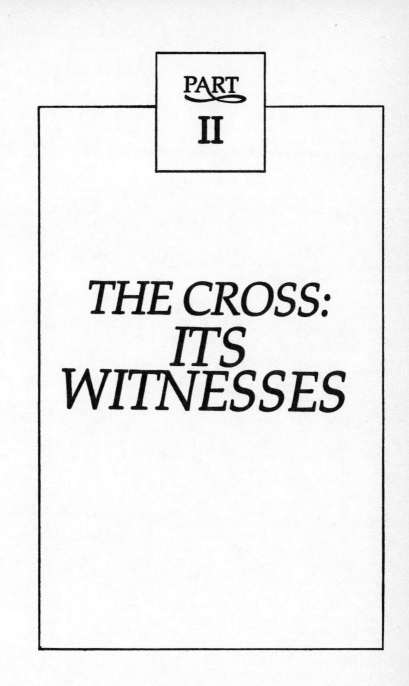

PART

II

*THE CROSS:
ITS
WITNESSES*

11

WHO WOULD HAVE BELIEVED?

*I*t's Friday morning. The news is blazing across the Jerusalem streets like a West Texas brush fire. "The Nazarene is being executed!" From Solomon's Porch to the Golden Gate people are passing the word. "Have you heard? They've got the Galilean." "I knew he would go too far." "They've got him? I don't believe it!" "They say one of his own men turned him in."

> Nicodemus is about to go AWOL.
> Graves are about to pop open.
> An earthquake is about to shake the city.
> The temple curtains are about to be torn in two.
> Shock, bewilderment, confusion.

A few weep. A few smile. A few walk up the hill to watch the spectacle. A few are irritated that the sanctity of the Passover is being violated by a bunch of social activists. Someone wonders aloud if this was the same man who was celebrated just a few days ago on a carpet of palm leaves. "A lot can happen in seven days," he comments.

A lot can happen in just one day.

Just ask Mary. Who could have convinced this mother yesterday that today would find her a few feet from the torn body of her son? And who could have convinced John on Thursday that he was twenty-four hours away from anointing the corpse of his hero? And Pilate? Who could have convinced Pilate that he was about to pass judgment on the Son of God!

A lot can happen in twenty-four hours.

Peter can tell you. If you had told this proud, devoted disciple yesterday that this morning would find him in the pit of guilt and shame, he would have proclaimed his loyalty. Or the other ten apostles can tell you. For them the same twenty-four hours brought both boasting and betrayal. And Judas . . . oh, pitiful Judas! Yesterday he was determined and defiant. This morning he is dead at his own belt. His dangling body eclipses the morning sun.

No one has been left untouched. No one.

The immensity of the Nazarene's execution makes it impossible to ignore. See the women arguing on the street corner? Lay odds that the subject is the Nazarene. Those two women at the market? They are giving their opinion on the self-proclaimed Messiah. The countless pilgrims who are entering Jerusalem for the Passover? They will go home with a spellbinding story of the "teacher who was raised from the dead." Everybody has an opinion. Everyone is choosing a side. You can't be neutral on an issue like this one. Apathy? Not this time. It's one side or the other. All have to choose.

And choose they did.

For every cunning Caiaphas there was a daring Nicodemus. For every cynical Herod there was a questioning Pilate. For every pot-mouthed thief there was a truth-seeking one. For every turncoat Judas there was a faithful John.

There was something about the crucifixion that made every witness either step toward it or away from it. It simultaneously compelled and repelled.

And today, two thousand years later, the same is true. It's the watershed. It's the Continental Divide. It's Normandy. And you are either on one side or the other. A choice is demanded. We can do what we want with the cross. We can examine its history. We can study its theology. We can reflect upon its prophecies. Yet the one thing we can't do is walk away in neutral. No fence sitting is permitted. The cross, in its absurd splendor, doesn't allow that. That is one luxury that God, in his awful mercy, doesn't permit.

On which side are you?

12

FACES IN THE CROWD

---

*T*wo types of people were touched by the cross: those touched by choice and those touched by chance. Among the latter, some intriguing tales are still told.

I

Take Malchus, for example. As a servant of the high priest, he was only doing his job at the Garden. Yet, this routine raid would have been his last if he had not been quick to duck. The torches gave just enough light for him to see the flash of the sword and "swoosh!" Malchus leans back enough to save his neck but not his ear. Peter gets a rebuke and Malchus gets a healing touch, and the event is history.

History, that is, to everyone but Malchus. Had it not been for the telltale bloodstain on his cloak, he might have awakened the next morning talking about a crazy dream he'd had. Some believe that Malchus was later numbered among the believers at Jerusalem. We don't know for sure. But we can be sure of one thing: from that night on, whenever Malchus would hear people talk about the carpenter who rose from the dead, he wouldn't scoff. No, he'd tug at his earlobe and know that it was possible.

II

It happened too fast. One minute Barabbas was in his cell on death row playing Tic-Tac-Toe on the dirt walls, and the next he was outside squinting his eyes at the bright sun.

"You're free to go."

Barabbas scratches his beard. "What?"

"You're free. They took the Nazarene instead of you."

Barabbas has often been compared to humanity, and rightly so. In many ways he stands for us: a prisoner who was freed because someone he had never seen took his place.

But I think Barabbas was probably smarter than we are in one respect.

As far as we know, he took his sudden freedom for what it was, an undeserved gift. Someone tossed him a life preserver and he grabbed it, no questions asked. You couldn't imagine him pulling some of our stunts. We take our free gift and try to earn it or diagnose it or pay for it instead of simply saying "thank you" and accepting it.

Ironic as it may appear, one of the hardest things to do is to be saved by grace. There's something in us that reacts to God's free gift. We have some weird compulsion to create laws, systems, and regulations that will make us "worthy" of our gift.

Why do we do that? The only reason I can figure is pride. To accept grace means to accept its necessity, and most folks don't like to do that. To accept grace also means that one realizes his despair, and most people aren't too keen on doing that either.

Barabbas, though, knew better. Hopelessly

stranded on death row, he wasn't about to balk at a granted stay of execution. Maybe he didn't understand mercy and surely he didn't deserve it, but he wasn't about to refuse it. We might do well to realize that our plight isn't too different than that of Barabbas's. We, too, are prisoners with no chance for appeal. But why some prefer to stay in prison while the cell door has been unlocked is a mystery worth pondering.

III

If it is true that a picture paints a thousand words, then there was a Roman centurion who got a dictionary full. All he did was see Jesus suffer. He never heard him preach or saw him heal or followed him through the crowds. He never witnessed him still the wind; he only witnessed the way he died. But that was all it took to cause this weather-worn soldier to take a giant step in faith. "Surely this was a righteous man."[1]

That says a lot, doesn't it? It says the rubber of faith meets the road of reality under hardship. It says the trueness of one's belief is revealed in pain. Genuineness and character are unveiled in misfortune. Faith is at its best, not in three-piece suits on Sunday mornings or at V.B.S. on summer days, but at hospital bedsides, cancer wards, and cemeteries.

Maybe that's what moved this old, crusty soldier. Serenity in suffering is a stirring testimony. Anybody can preach a sermon on a mount surrounded by daisies. But only one with a gut full of faith can *live* a sermon on a mountain of pain.

[1]Luke 23:47

13

WELL . . . ALMOST

Almost. It's a sad word in any man's dictionary. "Almost." It runs herd with "nearly," "next time," "if only," and "just about." It's a word that smacks of missed opportunities, aborted efforts, and fumbled chances. It's honorable mention, right field, on the bench, runner-up, and burnt cookies.

Almost. The one that got away. The sale that nearly closed. The gamble that almost paid off. Almost.

How many people do you know whose claim to fame is an almost?

"Did I ever tell you about the time I almost was selected as the Employee of the Year?

"They say he almost made the big leagues."

"I caught a catfish that was taller than me! Well . . . almost."

As long as there have been people, there have been almosts. People who *almost* won the battle, who *almost* climbed the mountain, who *almost* found the treasure.

One of the most famous "almost's" is found in the Bible. Pilate. Yet, what he missed was far more significant than a catfish or an award.

He almost performed what would have been history's greatest act of mercy. He almost pardoned the Prince of Peace. He almost released the Son of God. He almost opted to acquit the Christ. Almost. He had the power. He had the choice. He wore the signet ring. The option to free God's Son was his . . . and he did it . . . almost.

Almost. How many times do these six ugly letters find their way into despairing epitaphs?

"He almost got it together."

"She almost chose not to leave him."

"They almost tried one more time."

"We almost worked it out."

"He almost became a Christian."

What is it that makes *almost* such a potent word? Why is there such a wide gap between "he almost" and "he did"?

In the case of Pilate, we don't have to look far to find an answer. It is Dr. Luke's acute commentary in chapter 23 that provides the reason. Let's tune in at verse 22:

> A third time he [Pilate] said to them [the crowd], "Why, what evil has he done? I have found in him no crime deserving death; I will therefore chastise him and release him." But they were urgent, demanding with loud cries that he should be crucified. *And their voices prevailed* (italics mine, RSV).

You're right, Luke. *Their* voices prevailed. And, as a result, Pilate's pride prevailed. Pilate's fear prevailed. Pilate's power-hunger prevailed.

"Their" voices were not the only voices, you know. There were at least three others Pilate could have heard.

80

He could have heard the voice of Jesus. Pilate stood eye to eye with him. Five times he postponed the decision hoping to gratify the mob with policies or lashings.[2] Yet Jesus was always sent back to him. Three times he stood eye to eye with this compelling Nazarene who had come to reveal the truth. "What is truth?" Pilate asked rhetorically (or was it honestly?). Jesus' silence was much louder than the crowd's demands. But Pilate didn't listen.

He could have heard the voice of his wife. She pleaded with him to "have nothing to do with that righteous man for I have suffered much over him today in a dream."[1] One has to pause and wonder about the origin of such a dream that would cause a lady of purple to call a small-town Galilean righteous. But Pilate didn't.

Or he could have heard his own voice. Surely he could see through the facade. "Ananias, Caiaphas, cut the phoney allegiance, you slobs; I know where your interests are." Surely his conscience was speaking to him. "There is nothing wrong with this man. A bit mysterious maybe, but that's no reason to string him up."

He could have heard other voices. But he didn't. He almost did. But he didn't. Satan's voices prevailed.

His voice often does prevail. Have you heard his wooings?

"One time won't hurt."

"She'll never know."

"Other people do much worse things."

"At least you're not being hypocritical."

His rhetoric of rationalization never ends. The father of lies croons and woos like a traveling peddler, promising the moon and delivering disaster. "Step right up. Taste my brew of pleasure and sing my song of sensuality. After all, who knows about tomorrow?"

God, meanwhile, never enters a shouting match with Satan. Truth need not scream. He stands permanently, quietly pleading, ever present. No tricks, no side shows, no temptations, just open proof.

People's reactions vary. Some flow immediately to the peddler of poison. Others turn quickly to the Prince of Peace. Most of us, however, are caught somewhere in between, lingering on the edge of Satan's crowd yet hovering within earshot of the message of God.

Pilate learned the hard way that this stance of "almost" is suicidal. The other voices will win. Their lure is too strong. Their call too compelling. And Pilate also learned that there is no darker hell than the one of remorse. Washing your hands a thousand times won't free you from the guilt of an opportunity ignored. It's one thing to forgive yourself for something you did. It is something else to try to forgive yourself for something that you might have done, but didn't.

Jesus knew that all along. For our own good, he demanded and demands absolute obedience. He never has had room for "almost" in his vocabulary. You are either with him or against him. With Jesus "nearly" has to become "certainly." "Sometimes" has to become "always." "If only" has to become "regardless." And "next time" has to become "this time."

No, Jesus never had room for "almost" and he still doesn't. "Almost" may count in horseshoes and hand grenades, but with the Master, it is just as good as a "never."

[1]Matthew 27:19, RSV
[2]Luke 23:4, 7, 17, 20, 22

14

THE TEN WHO RAN

There is something striking in the simple fact that the disciples got together again. I mean, they had to have been embarrassed. As they sat gawking at each other that Sunday, they must have felt a bit foolish. Only two nights earlier the kitchen had gotten hot and they had taken off. It was as if someone threw a pan of scalding water on a bunch of cats. Bam! Off they scampered. They didn't stop until they had ducked into every available hole in Jerusalem.

Have you ever wondered what the disciples did that weekend? I have. I've wondered if any walked the streets or thought of going home. I've wondered what they said when people asked them what happened. "Uh ... well ... you see ..." I've wondered if they stayed in pairs or small groups or alone. I've wondered what they thought, what they felt.

"We had to run! They would have killed us all!"

"I don't understand what happened."

"I let him down."

"He should have warned us!"

I have wondered where they were when the sky turned black. I've wondered, were they near the temple when the curtain ripped or near the cemetery when the graves opened? I've wondered if any of them even dared to sneak back up to the hillside and stand at the edge of the crowd and stare at the three silhouettes on the hill.

No one knows. Those hours are left to speculation. Any guilt, any fear, any doubts are all unrecorded.

But we do know one thing. They came back. Slowly. One by one. They came back. Matthew, Nathaniel, Andrew. They came out of hiding. Out of the shadows. James, Peter, Thaddeus. Perhaps some were already on their way home, back to Galilee, but they turned around and came back. Perhaps others had given up in disgust, but they changed their minds. Maybe others were flooded with shame, but still they returned.

One by one, they appeared at that same upper room. (They must have been relieved to see others already there.)

From all sections of the city they appeared. Too convicted to go home, yet too confused to go on. Each with a desperate hope that it had all been a nightmare or a cruel joke. Each hoping to find some kind of solace in numbers. They came back. Something in their nature refused to let them give up. Something in those words spoken by the Master pulled them back together.

It certainly was an awkward position in which to be. Caught on that uneven ground between failure and forgiveness. Suspended somewhere between "I can't believe I did it" and "I'll never do it again." Too ashamed to ask for forgiveness, yet too loyal to give up. Too guilty to be counted in, but too faithful to be counted out.

I guess we've all been there. I dare say that all of us have witnessed our sandcastle promises swept away by the pouncing waves of panic and insecurity. I imagine that all of us have seen our words of promise and obedience ripped into ribbons by the chainsaw of fear and fright. And I haven't met a person yet who hasn't done the very thing he swore he would never do. We've all walked the streets of Jerusalem.

Why did the disciples come back? What made them return? Rumors of the resurrection? That had to be part of it. Those who walked next to Jesus had learned to expect him to do the unusual. They had seen him forgive a woman who had five husbands, honor a pint-size thief disguised as a tax collector, and love a streetwalker whose reputation would have brought blushes to the faces of Bonnie and Clyde. They'd seen him scare the devil out of some demoniacs and put the fear of God in some churchgoers. Traditions had tumbled, lepers had leaped, sinners had sung, Pharisees had fumed, multitudes had been moved. You just don't pack up the bags and go home after three years like that.

Maybe he really had risen from the dead.

But it was more than just rumors of an empty tomb that brought them back. There was something in their hearts that wouldn't let them live with their betrayal. For as responsible as their excuses were, they weren't good enough to erase the bottom line of the story: they had betrayed their Master. When Jesus needed them they had scampered. And now they were having to deal with the shame.

Seeking forgiveness, but not knowing where to look for it, they came back. They gravitated to that same upper room that contained the sweet memories of broken bread and symbolic wine. The simple fact that they returned says something about their leader. It says something about Jesus that those who knew him best could not stand to be in his disfavor. For the original twelve there were only two options—surrender or suicide. Yet, it also says something about Jesus that those who knew him best knew that although they had done exactly what they had promised they wouldn't, they could still find forgiveness.

So they came back. Each with a scrapbook full of memories and a thin thread of hope. Each knowing that it is all over, but in his heart hoping that the impossible will happen once more. "If I had just one more chance."

There they sat. What little conversation there is focuses on the rumors of an empty tomb. Someone sighs. Someone locks the door. Someone shuffles his feet.

And just when the gloom gets good and thick, just when their wishful thinking is falling victim to logic, just when someone says, "How I'd give my immortal soul to see him one more time," a familiar face walks through the wall.

My, what an ending. Or, better said, what a beginning! Don't miss the promise unveiled in this story. For those of us who, like the apostles, have turned and run when we should have stood and fought, this passage is pregnant with hope. A repentant heart is all he demands. Come out of the shadows! Be done with your hiding! A repentant heart is enough to summon the Son of God himself to walk through our walls of guilt and shame. He who forgave his followers stands ready to forgive the rest of us. All we have to do is come back.

No wonder they call him the Savior.

15

THE ONE WHO STAYED

I' ve always perceived John as a fellow who viewed life simply. "Right is right and wrong is wrong, and things aren't nearly as complicated as we make them out to be."

For example, defining Jesus would be a challenge to the best of writers, but John handles the task with casual analogy. The Messiah, in a word, was 'the Word.' A walking message. A love letter. Be he a fiery verb or a tender adjective, he was, quite simply, a word.

And life? Well, life is divided into two sections, light and darkness. If you are in one, you are not in the other and vice versa.

Next question?

"The devil is the father of lies and the Messiah is the father of truth. God is love and you are in his corner if you love, too. In fact, most problems are solved by loving one another."

And sometimes, when the theology gets a bit thick, John pauses just long enough to offer a word of explanation. Because of this patient storytelling, we have the classic commentary, "God so loved the world that he gave his one and only Son."

But I like John most for the way he loved Jesus. His relationship with Jesus was, again, rather simple. To John, Jesus was a good friend with a good heart and a good idea. A once-upon-a-time storyteller with a somewhere-over-the-rainbow promise.

One gets the impression that to John, Jesus was above all a loyal companion. Messiah? Yes. Son of God? Indeed. Miracle worker? That, too. But more than anything Jesus was a pal. Someone you could go camping with or bowling with or count the stars with.

Simple. To John, Jesus wasn't a treatise on social activism, nor was he a license for blowing up abortion clinics or living in a desert. Jesus was a friend.

Now what do you do with a friend? (Well, that's rather simple too.) You stick by him.

Maybe that is why John is the only one of the twelve who was at the cross. He came to say goodbye. By his own admission he hadn't quite put the pieces together yet. But that didn't really matter. As far as he was concerned, his closest friend was in trouble and he came to help.

"Can you take care of my mother?"

Of course. That's what friends are for.

John teaches us that the strongest relationship with Christ may not necessarily be a complicated one. He teaches us that the greatest webs of loyalty are spun, not with airtight theologies or foolproof philosophies, but with friendships; stubborn, selfless, joyful friendships.

After witnessing this stubborn love, we are left with a burning desire to have one like it. We are left feeling that if we could have been in anyone's sandals that day, we would have been in young John's and would have been the one to offer a smile of loyalty to this dear Lord.

16

THE HILL OF REGRET

While Jesus was climbing up the hill of Calvary, Judas was climbing another hill; the hill of regret.

He walked it alone. Its trail was rock-strewn with shame and hurt. Its landscape was as barren as his soul. Thorns of remorse tore at his ankles and calves. The lips that had kissed a king were cracked with grief. And on his shoulders he bore a burden that bowed his back—his own failure.

Why Judas betrayed his master is really not important. Whether motivated by anger or greed, the end result was the same—regret.

A few years ago I visited the Supreme Court. As I sat in the visitor's chambers, I observed the splendor of the scene. The chief justice was flanked by his colleagues. Robed in honor, they were the apex of justice. They represented the efforts of countless minds through thousands of decades. Here was man's best effort to deal with his own failures.

How pointless it would be, I thought to myself, if I approached the bench and requested forgiveness for my mistakes. Forgiveness for talking back to my fifth grade teacher. Forgiveness for being disloyal to my friends. Forgiveness for pledging "I won't" on Sunday and saying "I will" on Monday. Forgiveness for the countless hours I have spent wandering in society's gutters.

It would be pointless because the judge could do nothing. Maybe a few days in jail to appease my guilt, but forgiveness? It wasn't his to give. Maybe that's why so many of us spend so many hours on the hill of regret. We haven't found a way to forgive ourselves.

So up the hill we trudge. Weary, wounded hearts wrestling with unresolved mistakes. Sighs of anxiety. Tears of frustration. Words of rationalization. Moans of doubt. For some the pain is on the surface. For others the hurt is submerged, buried in a rarely touched substrata of bad memories. Parents, lovers, professionals. Some trying to forget, others trying to remember, all trying to cope. We walk silently in single file with leg irons of guilt. Paul was the man who posed the question that is on all of our lips, "Who will rescue me from this body of death?"[1]

At the trail's end there are two trees.

One is weathered and leafless. It is dead but still sturdy. Its bark is gone, leaving smooth wood bleached white by the years. Twigs and buds no longer sprout, only bare branches fork from the trunk. On the strongest of these branches is tied a hangman's noose. It was here that Judas dealt with his failure.

If only Judas had looked at the adjacent tree. It is also dead; its wood is also smooth. But there is no noose tied to its crossbeam. No more death on this tree. Once was enough. One death for all.

Those of us who have also betrayed Jesus know better than to be too hard on Judas for choosing the tree he did. To think that Jesus would really unburden our shoulders and unshackle our legs after all we've done to him is not easy to believe. In fact, it takes just as much faith to believe that Jesus can look past my betrayals as it does to believe that he rose from the dead. Both are just as miraculous.

What a pair, these two trees. Only a few feet from the tree of despair stands the tree of hope. Life so paradoxically close to death. Goodness within arm's reach of darkness. A hangman's noose and a life preserver swinging in the same shadow.

But here they stand.

One can't help but be a bit stunned by the inconceivability of it all. Why does Jesus stand on life's most barren hill and await me with outstretched, nail-pierced hands? A "crazy, holy grace" it has been called.[2] A type of grace that doesn't hold up to logic. But then I guess grace doesn't have to be logical. If it did, it wouldn't be grace.

[1]Romans 7:24
[2]Frederick Buechner, *The Sacred Journey*, p. 52, Harper and Row, 1982.

17

THE GOSPEL OF THE SECOND CHANCE

*I*t was like discovering the prize in a box of Cracker-jacks or spotting a little pearl in a box of buttons or stumbling across a ten dollar bill in a drawer full of envelopes.

It was small enough to overlook. Only two words. I know I'd read that passage a hundred times. But I'd never seen it. Maybe I'd passed over it in the excitement of the resurrection. Or, since Mark's account of the resurrection is by far the briefest of the four, maybe I'd just not paid too much attention. Or, maybe since it's in the last chapter of the gospel, my weary eyes had always read too quickly to note this little phrase.

But I won't miss it again. It's highlighted in yellow and underlined in red. You might want to do the same. Look in Mark, chapter 16. Read the first five verses about the womens' surprise when they find the stone moved to the side. Then feast on that beautiful phrase spoken by the angel, "He is not here, he is risen," but don't pause for too long. Go a bit further. Get your pencil ready and enjoy this jewel in the seventh verse (here it comes). The verse reads like this: "But go, tell his disciples and Peter that he is going before you to Galilee."

Did you see it? Read it again. (This time I italicized the words.)

"But go, tell his disciples *and Peter* that he is going before you to Galilee."

Now tell me if that's not a hidden treasure.

If I might paraphrase the words, "Don't stay here, go tell the disciples," a pause, then a smile, "and *especially* tell Peter, that he is going before you to Galilee."

What a line. It's as if all of heaven had watched Peter fall—and it's as if all of heaven wanted to help him back up again. "Be sure and tell Peter that he's not left out. Tell him that one failure doesn't make a flop."

Whew!

No wonder they call it the gospel of the second chance.

Not many second chances exist in the world today. Just ask the kid who didn't make the little league team or the fellow who got the pink slip or the mother of three who got dumped for a "pretty little thing."

Not many second chances. Nowadays it's more like, "It's now or never." "Around here we don't tolerate incompetence." "Gotta get tough to get along." "Not much room at the top." "Three strikes and you're out." "It's a dog-eat-dog world!"

Jesus has a simple answer to our masochistic mania. "It's a dog-eat-dog world?" he would say. "Then don't live with the dogs." That makes sense doesn't it? Why let a bunch of other failures tell you how much of a failure you are?

Sure you can have a second chance.

Just ask Peter. One minute he felt lower than a snake's belly and the next minute he was the high hog at the trough. Even the angels wanted this distraught net-caster to know that it wasn't over. The message came loud and clear from the celestial Throne Room through the divine courier. "Be sure and tell Peter that he gets to bat again."

Those who know these types of things say that the Gospel of Mark is really the transcribed notes and dictated thoughts of Peter. If this is true, then it was Peter himself who included these two words! And if these really are his words, I can't help but imagine that the old fisherman had to brush away a tear and swallow a lump when he got to this point in the story.

It's not every day that you get a second chance. Peter must have known that. The next time he saw Jesus, he got so excited that he barely got his britches on before he jumped into the cold water of the Sea of Galilee. It was also enough, so they say, to cause this backwoods Galilean to carry the gospel of the second chance all the way to Rome where they killed him. If you've ever wondered what would cause a man to be willing to be crucified upside down, maybe now you know.

It's not every day that you find someone who will give you a second chance—much less someone who will give you a second chance every day.

But in Jesus, Peter found both.

18

LEAVE ROOM FOR THE MAGIC

*T*homas. He defies tidy summary.

Oh, I know we've labeled him. Somewhere in some sermon somebody called him "Doubting Thomas." And the nickname stuck. And it's true, he *did* doubt. It's just that there was more to it than that. There was more to his questioning than a simple lack of faith. It was more due to a lack of imagination. You see it in more than just the resurrection story.

Consider, for instance, the time that Jesus was talking in all eloquence about the home he was going to prepare. Though the imagery wasn't easy for Thomas to grasp, he was doing his best. You can see his eyes filling his face as he tries to envision a big white house on St. Thomas Avenue. And just when Thomas is about to get the picture, Jesus assumes, "You know the way that I am going." Thomas blinks a time or two, looks around at the other blank faces, and then bursts out with candid aplomb, "Lord, we don't know where you are going, so how can we know the way?"[1] Thomas didn't mind speaking his mind. If you don't understand something, say so! His imagination would only stretch so far.

And then there was the time that Jesus told his disciples he was going to go be with Lazarus even though Lazarus was already dead and buried. Thomas couldn't imagine what Jesus was referring to, but if Jesus was wanting to go back into the arena with those Jews who had tried once before to stone him, Thomas wasn't going to let him face them alone. So he patted his trusty sidearm and said, "Let's die with him!"[2] Thomas had spent his life waiting on the Messiah, and now that the Messiah was here, Thomas was willing to spend his life for him. Not much imagination, but a lot of loyalty.

Perhaps it is this trait of loyalty that explains why Thomas wasn't in the Upper Room when Jesus appeared to the other apostles. You see, I think Thomas took the death of Jesus pretty hard. Even though he couldn't quite comprehend all the metaphors that Jesus at times employed, he was still willing to go to the end with him. But he had never expected that the end would come so abruptly and prematurely. As a result, Thomas was left with a crossword puzzle full of unanswered riddles.

On the one hand, the idea of a resurrected Jesus was too farfetched for dogmatic Thomas. His limited creativity left little room for magic or razzle dazzle. Besides, he wasn't about to set himself up to be disappointed again. One disappointment was enough, thank you. Yet, on the other hand, his loyalty made him yearn to believe. As long as there was the slimmest thread of hope, he wanted to be counted in.

His turmoil, then, came from a fusion between his lack of imagination and his unwavering loyalty. He was too honest with life to be gullible and yet was too loyal to Jesus to be unfaithful. In the end, it was this realistic devotion that caused him to utter the now famous condition, "Unless I see the nail marks in his hands and put my fingers where the nails were, I will not believe it."[3]

So, I guess you could say that he did doubt. But it was a different kind of doubting that springs not from timidity or mistrust, but from a reluctance to believe the impossible and a simple fear of being hurt twice.

Most of us are the same way, aren't we? In our world of budgets, long-range planning and computers, don't we find it hard to trust in the unbelievable? Don't most of us tend to scrutinize life behind furrowed brows and walk with cautious steps? It's hard for us to imagine that God can surprise us. To make a little room for miracles today, well, it's not sound thinking.

As a result, we, like Thomas, find it hard to believe that God can do the very thing that he is best at; replacing death with life. Our infertile imaginations bear little hope that the improbable will occur. We then, like Thomas, let our dreams fall victim to doubt.

We make the same mistake that Thomas made: we forget that "impossible" is one of God's favorite words.

How about you? How is your imagination these days? When was the last time you let some of your dreams elbow out your logic? When was the last time you imagined the unimaginable? When was the last time you dreamed of an entire world united in peace or all believers united in fellowship? When was the last time you dared dream of the day when every mouth will be fed and every nation dwell in peace? When was the last time you dreamed about every creature on earth hearing about the Messiah? Has it been awhile since you claimed God's promise to do "more than all we ask or imagine?"[4]

Though it went against every logical bone in his body, Thomas said he would believe if he could have just a little proof. And Jesus (who is ever so patient with our doubting), gave Thomas exactly what he requested. He extended his hands one more time. And was Thomas ever surprised. He did a double take, fell flat on his face, and cried, "My Lord and my God!"[5]

Jesus must have smiled.

He knew he had a winner in Thomas. Anytime you mix loyalty with a little imagination, you've got a man of God on your hands. A man who will die for a truth. Just look at Thomas. Legend has him hopping a freighter to India where they had to kill him to get him to quit talking about his home prepared in the world to come and his friend who came back from the dead.

[1]John 14:5 RSV
[2]John 11:16
[3]John 20:25, author's paraphrase.
[4]Ephesians 3:20
[5]John 20:28

19

A CANDLE
IN THE CAVERN

They are coming as friends—secret friends—but friends nonetheless. "You can take him down now, soldier. I'll take care of him."

The afternoon sun is high as they stand silently on the hill. It is much quieter than it was earlier. Most of the crowd has left. The two thieves gasp and groan as they hang near death. A soldier leans a ladder against the center tree, ascends it and removes the stake that holds the beam to the upright part of the cross. Two of the other soldiers, glad that the day's work is nearing completion, assist with the heavy chore of laying the cypress crosspiece and body on the ground.

"Careful now," says Joseph.

The five-inch nails are wrenched from the hard wood, freeing the limp hands. The body that encased a Savior is lifted and laid on a large rock.

"He's yours," says the sentry. The cross is set aside, soon to be carried into the supply room until it is needed again.

The two are not accustomed to this type of work. Yet their hands move quickly to their tasks.

Joseph of Arimathea kneels behind the head of Jesus and tenderly wipes the wounded face. With a soft, wet cloth he cleans the blood that came in the garden, that came from the lashings and from the crown of thorns. With this done, he closes the eyes tight.

Nicodemus unrolls some linen sheeting that Joseph brought and places it on the rock beside the body. The two Jewish leaders lift the lifeless body of Jesus and set it on the linen. Parts of the body are now anointed with perfumed spices. As Nicodemus touches the cheeks of the Master with aloe, the emotion he has been containing escapes. His own tear falls on the face of the crucified King. He pauses to brush away another. The middle-aged Jew looks longingly at the young Galilean.

It's a bit ironic that the burial of Jesus should be conducted, not by those who had boasted they would never leave, but by two members of the Sanhedrin—two representatives of the religious group that killed the Messiah.

But then again, of all who were indebted to this broken body, none were as much as those two. Many had been freed from the deep pits of slavery and sickness. Many had been found in the darkest of tunnels, tunnels of perversion and death. But no tunnel was ever darker than the tunnel from which these two had been rescued.

The tunnel of religion.

They don't come any darker. Its caverns are many and its pitfalls are deep. Its subterranean stench reeks with the spirit of good intentions. Its endless maze of channels are cluttered with the disoriented. Its paths are covered with cracked wineskins and spilt wine.

You wouldn't want to carry a young faith into this tunnel. Young minds probing with questions quickly stale in the numbing darkness. Fresh insights are squelched in order to protect fragile traditions. Originality is discouraged. Curiosity is stifled. Priorities are re-shuffled.

Christ had nothing but stinging words of rebuke for those who dwell in the caverns. "Hypocrites," he called them. Godless actors. Fence builders. Inflexible judges. Unauthorized hedge trimmers. Hair splitters. "Blind guides." "White-washed tombs." "Snakes." "Vipers." Bang! Bang! Bang! Jesus had no room for those who specialized in making religion a warlord, and faith a foot-race. No room at all.[1]

Joseph and Nicodemus were tired of it, too. They had seen it for themselves. They had seen the list of rules and regulations. They had watched the people tremble under unbearable burdens. They had heard the hours of senseless wrangling over legalistic details. They had worn the robes and sat at the places of honor and seen the word of God be made void. They had seen religion become the crutch that cripples.

And they wanted out.

It was a sizable risk. The high society of Jerusalem wasn't going to look too kindly on two of their religious leaders burying a revolutionist. But for Joseph and Nicodemus the choice was obvious. The stories this young preacher from Nazareth told rang with the truth that they had never heard in the cavern. And, besides, they'd much rather save their souls than their skin.

So they lifted the body slowly and carried it to the unused tomb. In so doing, they lit a candle in the cavern.

Supposing these two have been observing the religious world during the last two thousand years, they have probably found things to be not too terribly different. There is still a sizable amount of evil that wears the robe of religion and uses the Bible as a sledgehammer. It is still fashionable to have sacred titles and wear holy chains. And it is still often the case that one has to find faith in spite of the church instead of in the church.

But they have also observed that just when the religious get too much religion and the righteous get too right, God finds somebody in the cavern who will light a candle. It was lit by Luther at Wittenburg, by Latimer in London, and by Tyndale in Germany. John Knox fanned the flame as a galley slave and Alexander Campbell did the same as a preacher.

It's not easy to light a candle in a dark cavern. Yet, those of us whose lives have been enlightened because of these courageous men are eternally grateful. And of all the acts of enlightenment, there is no doubt which one was the noblest.

"You can take him down now, soldier. I'll take care of him."

[1]Matthew 23

20

MINIATURE MESSENGERS

*B*efore we bid goodbye to those present at the cross, I
have one more introduction to make. This introduction is very special.

There was one group in attendance that day whose role was critical. They didn't speak much, but they were there. Few noticed them, but that's not surprising. Their very nature is so silent they are often overlooked. In fact, the gospel writers scarcely gave them a reference. But we know they were there. They had to be. They had a job to do.

Yes, this representation did much more than witness the divine drama; they expressed it. They captured it. They displayed the despair of Peter; they betrayed the guilt of Pilate and unveiled the anguish of Judas. They transmitted John's confusion and translated Mary's compassion.

Their prime role, however, was with that of the Messiah. With utter delicacy and tenderness, they offered relief to his pain and expression to his yearning.

Who am I describing? You may be surprised.

Tears.

Those tiny drops of humanity. Those round, wet balls of fluid that tumble from our eyes, creep down our cheeks, and splash on the floor of our hearts. They were there that day. They are always present at such times. They should be, that's their job. They are miniature messengers; on call twenty-four hours a day to substitute for crippled words. They drip, drop, and pour from the corner of our souls, carrying with them the deepest emotions we possess. They tumble down our faces with announcements that range from the most blissful joy to darkest despair.

The principle is simple; when words are most empty, tears are most apt.

A tearstain on a letter says much more than the sum of all its words. A tear falling on a casket says what a spoken farewell never could. What summons a mother's compassion and concern more quickly than a tear on a child's cheek? What gives more support than a sympathetic tear on the face of a friend?

Words failed the day the Savior was slain. They failed miserably. What words could have been uttered? What phrases could have possibly expressed the feelings of those involved?

That task, my friend, was left for the tears.

What do you do when words won't come? When all the nouns and verbs lay deflated at your feet, with what do you communicate? When even the loftiest statements stumble, what do you do? Are you one of the fortunate who isn't ashamed to let a tear take over? Can you be so happy that your eyes water and your throat swells? Can you be so proud that your pupils blur and your vision mists? And in sorrow, do you let your tears decompress that tight chest and untie that knot in your throat?

106

Or do you reroute your tears and let them only fall on the inside?

Not many of us are good at showing our feelings, you know. Especially us fellows. Oh, we can yell and curse and smoke, yessir! But tears? "Save those for the weak-kneed and timid. I've got a world to conquer!"

We would do well, guys, to pause and look at the tearstained faces that appear at the cross.

Peter. The burly fisherman. Strong enough to yank a full net out of the sea. Brave enough to weather the toughest storm. The man who only hours before had bared his sword against the entire Roman guard. But now look at him. Weeping, no . . . *wailing*. Huddled in a corner with his face hidden in his calloused hands. Would a real man be doing this? Admitting his fault? Confessing his failure? Begging forgiveness? Or would a real man bottle it up . . . justify it . . . rationalize it . . . keep a "stiff upper lip" and stand his ground? Has Peter lost his manhood? We know better don't we? Maybe he's less a man of the world, but less a man of God? No way.

And John, look at his tears. His face swollen with sorrow as he stands eye-level with the bloody feet of his Master. Is his emotion a lack of courage? Is his despair a lack of guts?

And the tears of Jesus. They came in the garden. I'm sure they came on the cross. Are they a sign of weakness? Do those stains on his cheeks mean he had no fire in his belly or grit in his gut?

Of course not.

Here's the point. It's not just tears that are the issue, it's what they represent. They represent the heart, the spirit, and the soul of a person. To put a lock and key on your emotions is to bury part of your Christ-likeness!

Especially when you come to Calvary.

You can't go to the cross with just your head and not your heart. It doesn't work that way. Calvary is not a mental trip. It's not an intellectual exercise. It's not a divine calculation or a cold theological principle.

It's a heart-splitting hour of emotion.

Don't walk away from it dry-eyed and unstirred. Don't just straighten your tie and clear your throat. Don't allow yourself to descend Calvary cool and collected.

Please . . . pause. Look again.

Those are nails in those hands.

That's *God* on that cross.

It's us who put him there.

Peter knew it. John knew it. Mary knew it.

They knew a great price was being paid. They knew who really pierced his side. They also somehow knew that history was being remade.

That's why they wept.

They *saw* the Savior.

God, may we never be so "educated," may we never be so "mature," may we never be so "religious" that we can see your passion without tears.

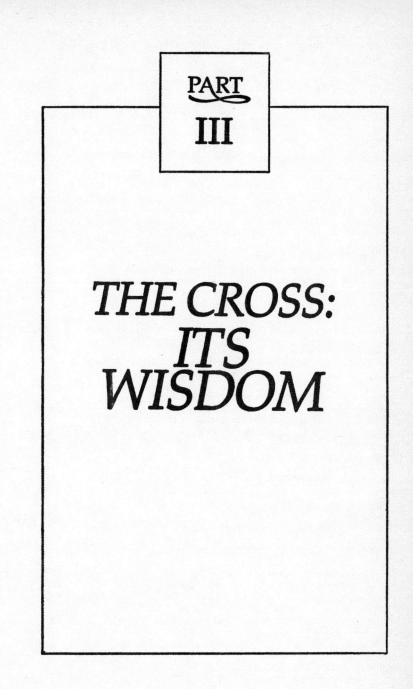

PART
III

THE CROSS: ITS WISDOM

21

ALIVE

Road. Dark. Stars. Shadows. Four. Sandals. Robes. Quiet. Suspense. Grove. Trees. Alone. Questions. Anguish. "Father!" Sweat. God. Man. God-Man. Prostrate. Blood. "NO!" "Yes." Angels. Comfort.

Footsteps. Torches. Voices. Romans. Surprise. Swords. Kiss. Confusion. Betrayal. Fearful. Run! Bound. Wrists. Marching.

Courtyard. Priests. Lamps. Sanhedrin. Caiaphas. Sneer. Silk. Arrogance. Beard. Plotting. Barefoot. Rope. Calm. Shove. Kick. Annas. Indignant. Messiah? Trial. Nazarene. Confident. Question. Answer. Punch!

Peter. "Me?" Rooster. Thrice. Guilt.

Proceedings. Court. Rejection. Prosecute. Weary. Pale. Witnesses. Liars. Inconsistent. Silence. Stares. "Blasphemer!" Anger. Waiting. Bruised. Dirty. Fatigued. Guards. Spit. Blindfold. Mocking. Blows. Fire. Twilight.

Sunrise. Golden. Jerusalem. Temple. Passover. Lambs. Lamb. Worshippers. Priests. Messiah. Hearing. Fraud. Prisoner. Waiting. Standing. Shifting. Strategy. "Pilate!" Trap. Murmurs. Exit.

Stirring. Parade. Crowd. Swell. Romans. Pilate. Toga. Annoyed. Nervous. Officers. Tunics. Spears. Silence. "Charge?" "Blasphemy." Indifference. Ignore. (Wife. Dream.) Worry. Interview. Lips. Pain, Determined. "King?" "Heaven." "Truth." "Truth?" Sarcasm. (Fear) "Innocent!" Roar. Voices. "Galilean!" "Galilee?" "Herod!"

9:00 A.M. Marchers. Palace. Herod. Fox. Schemer. Paunchy. Crown. Cape. Scepter. Hall. Elegance. Silence. Manipulate. Useless. Vexed. Revile. Taunt. "King?" Robe. Theatrical. Cynical. Hateful. "Pilate!"

Marching. Uproar. Prisoner. Hushed. Pilate. "Innocent!" Bedlam. "Barabbas!" Riot. Despair. Christ. Bare. Rings. Wall. Back. Whip. Slash. Scourge. Tear. Bone. Moan. Flesh. Rhythm. Silence. Whip! Silence. Whip! Silence. Whip! Thorns. Stinging. Blind. Laughter. Jeering. Scepter. Slap. Governor. Distraught. (Almost). Eyes. Jesus. Decision. Power. Freedom? Threats. Looks. Yelling. Weak. Basin. Water. Swayed. Compromise. Blood. Guilt.

Soldiers. Thieves. Crosspiece. Shoulder. Heavy. Beam. Heavy. Sun. Stagger. Incline. Houses. Shops. Faces. Mourners. Murmurs. Pilgrims. Women. Tumble. Cobblestone. Exhaustion. Gasping. Simon. Pathetic. Golgotha.

Skull. Calvary. Crosses. Execution. Death. Noon. Tears. Observers. Wails. Wine. Nude. Bruised. Swollen. Crossbeam. Sign. Ground. Nails. Pound. Pound. Pound. Pierced. Contorted. Thirst. Terrible. Grace. Writhing. Raised. Mounted. Hung. Suspended. Spasms. Heaving. Sarcasm. Sponge. Tears. Taunts. Forgiveness. Dice. Gambling. Darkness.

Absurdity.

Death. Life.

Pain. Peace.

Condemn. Promise.

Nowhere. Somewhere.

Him. Us.

"Father!" Robbers. Paradise. Wailing. Weeping. Stunned. "Mother." Compassion. Darkness. "My God!" Afraid. Scapegoat. Wilderness. Vinegar. "Father." Silence. Sigh. Death. Relief.

Earthquake. Cemetery. Tombs. Bodies. Mystery. Curtain. Spear. Blood. Water. Spices. Linen. Tomb. Fear. Waiting. Despair. Stone. Mary. Running. Maybe? Peter. John. Belief. Enlightenment. Truth. Mankind. Alive. Alive. Alive!

22

OPEN ARMS

*T*hey aren't exactly what you'd call a list of "Who's Who in Purity and Sainthood." In fact, some of their antics and attitudes would make you think of the Saturday night crowd at the county jail. What few halos there are among this befuddled bunch could probably use a bit of straightening and polish. Yet, strange as it may seem it is this very humanness that makes these people refreshing. They are so refreshing that should you ever need a reminder of God's tolerance, you'd find it in these people. If you ever wonder how in the world God could use you to change the world, look at these people.

What people? The people God used to change history. A ragbag of ne'er-do-wells and has-beens who found hope, not in their performance, but in God's proverbially open arms.

Let's start with Abraham. Though eulogized by Paul for his faith, this Father of a Nation wasn't without his weaknesses. He had a fibbing tongue that wouldn't stop! One time, in order to save his neck, he let the word get out that Sarah wasn't his wife but his sister, which was only half true.[1] And then, not long later, he did it again! "And Abraham said of Sarah his wife, 'She is my sister.'"[2]

Twice he traded in his integrity for security. That's what you call confidence in God's promises? Can you build a nation on that kind of faith? God can. God took what was good and forgave what was bad and used "old forked tongue" to start a nation.

Another household name is Moses. Definitely one of history's greatest. But until he was eighty years old he looked like he wouldn't amount to much more than a once-upon-a-time prince turned outlaw. Would you choose a wanted murderer to lead a nation out of bondage? Would you call upon a fugitive to carry the Ten Commandments? God did. And he called him, of all places, right out of the sheep pasture. Called his name through a burning bush. Scared old Moses right out of his shoes! There, with knees knocking and "Who me?" written all over his face, Moses agreed to go back into the ring.

And what can you say about a fellow whose lust got so lusty that he got a woman pregnant, tried to blame it on her husband, had her husband killed, and then went on living like nothing ever happened? Well, you could say he was a man after God's own heart. David's track record left a little to be desired, but his repentant spirit was unquestionable.

Then comes Jonah. God's ambassador to Nineveh. Jonah, however, had other ideas. He had no desire to go to that heathen city. So he hopped on another boat while God wasn't looking (or at least that's what Jonah thought). God put him in a whale's belly to bring him back to his senses. But even the whale couldn't stomach this missionary for too long. A good burp and Jonah went flying over the surf and landed big-eyed and repentant on the beach. (Which just goes to show that you can't keep a good man down.)

And on and on the stories go: Elijah, the prophet who pouted; Solomon, the king who knew too much; Jacob, the wheeler-dealer; Gomer, the prostitute; Sarah, the woman who giggled at God. One story after another of God using man's best and overcoming man's worst.

Even the genealogy of Jesus is salted with a dubious character or two—Tamar the adulteress, Rahab the harlot, and Bathsheba, who tended to take baths in questionable locations.

The reassuring lesson is clear. God used (and uses!) people to change the world. *People!* Not saints or superhumans or geniuses, but people. Crooks, creeps, lovers, and liars—he uses them all. And what they may lack in perfection, God makes up for in love.

Jesus later summarized God's stubborn love with a parable. He told about a teenager who decided that life at the farm was too slow for his tastes. So with pockets full of inheritance money, he set out to find the big time. What he found instead were hangovers, fair-weather friends, and long unemployment lines. When he had had just about as much of the pig's life as he could take, he swallowed his pride, dug his hands deep into his empty pockets, and began the long walk home; all the while rehearsing a speech that he planned to give to his father.

He never used it. Just when he got to the top of the hill, his father, who'd been waiting at the gate, saw him. The boy's words of apology were quickly muffled by the father's words of forgiveness. And the boy's weary body fell into his father's opened arms.

The same open arms welcomed him that had welcomed Abraham, Moses, David, and Jonah. No wagging fingers. No clenched fists. No "I told you so!" slaps or "Where have you been?" interrogations. No crossed arms.

119

No black eyes or fat lips. No. Only sweet, open arms. If you ever wonder how God can use you to make a difference in your world, just look at those he has already used and take heart. Look at the forgiveness found in those open arms and take courage.

And, by the way, never were those arms opened so wide as they were on the Roman cross. One arm extending back into history and the other reaching into the future. An embrace of forgiveness offered for anyone who'll come. A hen gathering her chicks. A father receiving his own. A redeemer redeeming the world.

No wonder they call him the Savior.

[1]Genesis 12:10-20
[2]Genesis 20:2

A STREET VENDOR NAMED CONTENTMENT

*A*hhh ... an hour of contentment. A precious moment of peace. A few minutes of relaxation. Each of us has a setting in which contentment pays a visit.

Early in the morning while the coffee is hot and everyone else is asleep.

Late at night as you kiss your six-year-old's sleepy eyes.

In a boat on a lake when memories of a life well-lived are vivid.

In the companionship of a well-worn, dogeared, even tearstained Bible.

In the arms of a spouse.

At Thanksgiving dinner or sitting near the Christmas tree.

An hour of contentment. An hour when deadlines are forgotten and strivings have ceased. An hour when what we have overshadows what we want. An hour when we realize that a lifetime of blood-sweating and headhunting can't give us what the cross gave us in one day—a clean conscience and a new start.

But unfortunately, in our squirrel cages of schedules, contests, and side-glancing, hours like these are about as common as one-legged monkeys. In our world, contentment is a strange street vendor, roaming, looking for a home, but seldom finding an open door. This old salesman moves slowly from house to house, tapping on windows, knocking on doors, offering his wares: an hour of peace, a smile of acceptance, a sigh of relief. But his goods are seldom taken. We are too busy to be content. (Which is crazy, since the reason we kill ourselves today is because we think it will make us content tomorrow).

"Not now, thank you. I've too much to do," we say. "Too many marks to be made, too many achievements to be achieved, too many dollars to be saved, too many promotions to be earned. And besides, if I'm content, someone might think I've lost my ambition."

So the street vendor named Contentment moves on. When I asked him why so few welcomed him into their homes, his answer left me convicted. "I charge a high price, you know. My fee is steep. I ask people to trade in their schedules, frustrations, and anxieties. I demand that they put a torch to their fourteen- hour days and sleepless nights. You'd think I'd have more buyers." He scratched his beard, then added pensively, "But people seem strangely proud of their ulcers and headaches."

Can I say something a bit personal? I'd like to give a testimony. A live one. I'm here to tell you that I welcomed this bearded friend into my living room this morning.

It wasn't easy.

My list of things was, for the most part, undone. My responsibilities were just as burdensome as ever. Calls to be made. Letters to be written. Checkbooks to be balanced.

But a funny thing happened on the way to the rat race that made me slip into neutral. Just as I got my sleeves rolled up, just as the old engine was starting to purr, just as I was getting up a good head of steam, my infant daughter, Jenna, needed to be held. She had a stomachache. Mom was in the bath so it fell to Daddy to pick her up.

She's three weeks old today. At first I started trying to do things with one hand and hold her with the other. You're smiling. You've tried that too? Just when I realized that it was impossible, I also realized that it was not at all what I was wanting to do.

I sat down and held her tight little tummy against my chest. She began to relax. A big sigh escaped her lungs. Her whimpers became gurgles. She slid down my chest until her little ear was right on top of my heart. That's when her arms went limp and she fell asleep.

And that's when the street vendor knocked at my door.

Goodbye, schedule. See you later, routine. Come back tomorrow, deadlines . . . hello Contentment, come on in.

So here we sit, Contentment, my daughter, and I. Pen in hand, note pad on Jenna's back. She'll never remember this moment and I'll never forget it. The sweet fragrance of a moment captured fills the room. The taste of an opportunity seized sweetens my mouth. The sunlight of a lesson learned illuminates my understanding. This is one moment that didn't get away.

The tasks? They'll get done. The calls? They'll get made. The letters? They'll be written. And you know what? They'll get done with a smile.

I don't do this enough, but I'm going to do it more. In fact, I'm thinking of giving that street vendor a key to my door. "By the way, Contentment, what are you doing this afternoon?"

24

CLOSE TO THE CROSS— BUT FAR FROM CHRIST

*T*here was some dice-throwing that went on at the foot of the cross.

Imagine this scene. The soldiers are huddled in a circle, their eyes turned downward. The criminal above them is forgotten. They gamble for some used clothes. The tunic, the cloak, the sandals are all up for grabs. Each soldier lays his luck on the hard earth, hoping to expand his wardrobe at the expense of a cross-killed carpenter.

I've wondered what that scene must have looked like to Jesus. As he looked downward past his bloody feet at the circle of gamblers, what did he think? What emotions did he feel? He must have been amazed. Here are common soldiers witnessing the world's most uncommon event and they don't even know it. As far as they're concerned, it's just another Friday morning and he is just another criminal. "Come on, hurry up; it's my turn!"

"All right, all right—this throw is for the sandals."

Casting lots for the possessions of Christ. Heads ducked. Eyes downward. Cross forgotten.

The symbolism is striking. Do you see it?

It makes me think of us. The religious. Those who claim heritage at the cross. I'm thinking of all of us. Every believer in the land. The stuffy. The loose. The strict. The simple. Upper church. Lower church. "Spirit-filled." Millenialists. Evangelical. Political. Mystical. Literal. Cynical. Robes. Collars. Three-piece suits. Born-againers. Ameners.

I'm thinking of us.

I'm thinking that we aren't so unlike those soldiers. (I'm sorry to say.)

We, too, play games at the foot of the cross. We compete for members. We scramble for status. We deal out judgments and condemnations. Competition. Selfishness. Personal gain. It's all there. We don't like what the other did so we take the sandal we won and walk away in a huff.

So close to the timber yet so far from the blood.

We are so close to the world's most uncommon event, but we act like common crapshooters huddled in bickering groups and fighting over silly opinions.

How many pulpit hours have been wasted on preaching the trivial? How many churches have tumbled at the throes of miniscuity? How many leaders have saddled their pet peeves, drawn their swords of bitterness and launched into battle against brethren over issues that are not worth discussing?

So close to the cross but so far from the Christ.

We specialize in "I am right" rallies. We write books about what the other does wrong. We major in finding gossip and become experts in unveiling weaknesses. We split into little huddles and then, God forbid, we split again.

Another name. Another doctrine. Another "error." Another denomination. Another poker game. Our Lord must be amazed.

"Those selfish soldiers," we smirk with our thumbs in lapels. "They were so close to the cross and yet so far from the Christ." And yet, are we so different? Our divisions are so numerous that we can't be cataloged. There are so many offshoots that even the offshoots have shoots!

Now . . . really.

Are our differences that divisive? Are our opinions that obtrusive? Are our walls that wide? Is it *that* impossible to find a common cause?

"May they all be one," Jesus prayed.

One. Not one in groups of two thousand. But one in One. *One* church. *One* faith. *One* Lord. Not Baptist, not Methodist, not Adventist. Just Christians. No denominations. No hierarchies. No traditions. Just Christ.

Too idealistic? Impossible to achieve? I don't think so. Harder things have been done, you know. For example, once upon a tree, a Creator gave his life for his creation. Maybe all we need are a few hearts that are willing to follow suit.

What about you? Can you build a bridge? Toss a rope? Span a chasm? Pray for oneness? Can you be the soldier who snaps to his senses, jumps to his feet, and reminds the rest of us, "Hey, that's God on that cross!"

The similarity between the soldier's game and our game is scary. What did Jesus think? What does he think today? There is still dice-throwing going on. And it is at the foot of the cross.

25

THE FOG OF
THE BROKEN HEART

The fog of the broken heart.

It's a dark fog that slyly imprisons the soul and refuses easy escape. It's a silent mist that eclipses the sun and beckons the darkness. It's a heavy cloud that honors no hour and respects no person. Depression, discouragement, disappointment, doubt . . . all are companions of this dreaded presence.

The fog of the broken heart disorients our life. It makes it hard to see the road. Dim your lights. Wipe off the windshield. Slow down. Do what you wish, nothing helps. When this fog encircles us, our vision is blocked and tomorrow is a forever away. When this billowy blackness envelops us, the most earnest words of help and hope are but vacant phrases.

If you have ever been betrayed by a friend, you know what I mean. If you have ever been dumped by a spouse or abandoned by a parent, you have seen this fog. If you have ever placed a spade of dirt on a loved one's casket or kept vigil at a dear one's bedside, you, too, recognize this cloud.

If you have been in this fog, or are in it now, you can be sure of one thing—you are not alone. Even the saltiest of sea captains have lost their bearings because of the appearance of this unwanted cloud. Like the comedian said, "If broken hearts were commercials, we'd all be on TV."

Think back over the last two or three months. How many broken hearts did you encounter? How many wounded spirits did you witness? How many stories of tragedy did you read about?

My own reflection is sobering:

> The woman who lost her husband and son in a freak car wreck.
>
> The attractive mother of three who was abandoned by her husband.
>
> The child who was hit and killed by a passing garbage truck as he was getting off the school bus. His mother, who was waiting for him, witnessed the tragedy.
>
> The parents who found their teenager dead in the forest behind their home. He had hung himself from a tree with his own belt.

The list goes on and on, doesn't it? Foggy tragedies. How they blind our vision and destroy our dreams. Forget any great hopes of reaching the world. Forget any plans of changing society. Forget any aspirations of moving mountains. Forget all that. Just help me make it through the night!

The suffering of the broken heart.

Go with me for a moment to witness what was perhaps the foggiest night in history. The scene is very simple; you'll recognize it quickly. A grove of twisted olive trees. Ground cluttered with large rocks. A low stone fence. A dark, dark night.

Now, look into the picture. Look closely through the shadowy foliage. See that person? See that solitary figure? What's he doing? Flat on the ground. Face stained with dirt and tears. Fists pounding the hard earth. Eyes wide with a stupor of fear. Hair matted with salty sweat. Is that blood on his forehead?

That's Jesus. Jesus in the Garden of Gethsemane.

Maybe you've seen the classic portrait of Christ in the garden. Kneeling beside a big rock. Snow-white robe. Hands peacefully folded in prayer. A look of serenity on his face. Halo over his head. A spotlight from heaven illuminating his golden-brown hair.

Now, I'm no artist, but I can tell you one thing. The man who painted that picture didn't use the gospel of Mark as a pattern. Look what Mark wrote about that painful night.

> When they reached a place called Gethsemane, he said to his disciples, "Sit here while I pray." And he took Peter and James and John with him. Horror and dismay came over him, and he said to them, "My heart is ready to break with grief; stop here, and stay awake." Then he went forward a little, threw himself on the ground, and prayed that, if it were possible, this hour might pass him by. "Abba, Father," he said, "all things are possible to thee; take this cup away from me. Yet not what I will, but what thou wilt."
> He came back and found them asleep; and he said to Peter, "Asleep, Simon? Were you not able awake for one hour? Stay awake,

all of you; and pray that you may be spared the test. The spirit is willing, but the flesh is weak." Once more he went away and prayed. On his return he found them asleep again, for their eyes were heavy; and they did not know how to answer him.
The third time he came and said to them, "Still sleeping? Still taking your ease? Enough! The hour has come. The Son of Man is betrayed to sinful men. Up, let us go forward! My betrayer is upon us."

Look at those phrases. *"Horror* and *dismay* came over him." "My heart is ready to *break* with grief." "He went a little forward and *threw* himself on the ground."

Does this look like the picture of a saintly Jesus resting in the palm of God? Hardly. Mark used black paint to describe this scene. We see an agonizing, straining, and struggling Jesus. We see a "man of sorrows."[2] We see a man struggling with fear, wrestling with commitments, and yearning for relief.

We see Jesus in the fog of a broken heart.

The writer of Hebrews would later pen, "During the days of Jesus' life on earth, he offered up prayers and petitions with *loud cries and tears* to the one who could save him from death."[3]

My, what a portrait! Jesus is in pain. Jesus is on the stage of fear. Jesus is cloaked, not in sainthood, but in humanity.

The next time the fog finds you, you might do well to remember Jesus in the garden. The next time you think that no one understands, reread the fourteenth chapter of Mark. The next time your self-pity convinces you that no one cares, pay a visit to Gethsemane. And the next time you wonder if God really perceives the pain that prevails on this dusty planet, listen to him pleading among the twisted trees.

Here's my point. Seeing God like this does wonders for our own suffering. God was never more human than at this hour. God was never nearer to us than when he hurt. The Incarnation was never so fulfilled as in the garden.

As a result, time spent in the fog of pain could be God's greatest gift. It could be the hour that we finally see our Maker. If it is true that in suffering God is most like man, maybe in our suffering we can see God like never before.

The next time you are called to suffer, pay attention. It may be the closest you'll ever get to God. Watch closely. It could very well be that the hand that extends itself to lead you out of the fog is a pierced one.

[1]Mark 14:32-42
[2]Isaiah 53:3
[3]Hebrews 5:7, italics mine.

26

PÃO, SENHOR?

He couldn't have been over six years old. Dirty face, barefooted, torn T-shirt, matted hair. He wasn't too different from the other hundred thousand or so street orphans that roam Rio de Janeiro.

I was walking to get a cup of coffee at a nearby cafe when he came up behind me. With my thoughts somewhere between the task I had just finished and the class I was about to teach, I scarcely felt the tap, tap, tap on my hand. I stopped and turned. Seeing no one, I continued on my way. I'd only taken a few steps, however, when I felt another insistent tap, tap, tap. This time I stopped and looked downward. There he stood. His eyes were whiter because of his grubby cheeks and coal-black hair.

"Pão, senhor?" ("Bread, sir?")

Living in Brazil, one has daily opportunities to buy a candy bar or sandwich for these little outcasts. It's the least one can do. I told him to come with me and we entered the sidewalk cafe. "Coffee for me and something tasty for my little friend." The boy ran to the pastry counter and made his choice. Normally, these youngsters take the food and scamper back out into the street without a word. But this little fellow surprised me.

The cafe consisted of a long bar: one end for pastries and the other for coffee. As the boy was making his choice, I went to the other end of the bar and began drinking my coffee. Just as I was getting my derailed train of thought back on track, I saw him again. He was standing in the cafe entrance, on tiptoe, bread in hand, looking in at the people. "What's he doing?" I thought.

Then he saw me and scurried in my direction. He came and stood in front of me about eye-level with my belt buckle. The little Brazilian orphan looked up at the big American missionary, smiled a smile that would have stolen your heart and said, "Obrigado." (Thank you.) Then, nervously scratching the back of his ankle with his big toe, he added, "*Muito* obrigado." (Thank you *very much*.)

All of a sudden, I had a crazy craving to buy him the whole restaurant.

But before I could say anything, he turned and scampered out the door.

As I write this, I'm still standing at the coffee bar, my coffee is cold, and I'm late for my class. But I still feel the sensation that I felt half an hour ago. And I'm pondering this question: If I am so moved by a street orphan who says thank you for a piece of bread, how much more is God moved when I pause to thank him—really thank him—for saving my soul?

27

PUPPIES, BUTTERFLIES, AND A SAVIOR

When I was ten years old, I had a puppy named Tina. You would have loved her. She was the perfect pet. An irresistible, pug-nosed Pekingese pup. One ear fell over and the other ear stood straight up. She never tired of playing and yet never got in the way.

Her mother died when she was born so the rearing of the puppy fell to me. I fed her milk from a doll bottle and used to sneak out at night to see if she was warm. I'll never forget the night I took her to bed with me only to have her mess on my pillow. We made quite a pair. My first brush with parenthood.

One day I went into the backyard to give Tina her dinner. I looked around and spotted her in a corner near the fence. She had cornered a butterfly (as much as a butterfly can be cornered) and was playfully yelping and jumping in the air trying to catch the butterfly in her mouth. Amused, I watched her for a few minutes and then called to her.

"Tina! Come here, girl! It's time to eat!"

What happened next surprised me. Tina stopped her playing and looked at me. But instead of immediately scampering in my direction, she sat back on her haunches. Then she tilted her head back toward the butterfly, looked back at me, then back to the butterfly, and then back to me. For the first time in her life, she had to make a decision.

Her "want to" longed to pursue the butterfly which tauntingly awaited her in midair. Her "should" knew she was supposed to obey her master. A classic struggle of the will: a war between the "want" and the "should." The same question that has faced every adult now faced my little puppy.

And do you know what she did? She chased the butterfly! Scurrying and barking, she ignored my call and chased that silly thing until it flew over the fence.

That is when the guilt hit.

She stopped at the fence for a long time, sitting back on her hind legs looking up in the air where the butterfly had made its exit. Slowly, the excitement of the chase was overshadowed by the guilt of disobedience.

She turned painfully and walked back to encounter her owner. (To be honest, I was a little miffed.) Her head was ducked as she regretfully trudged across the yard.

For the first time in her life, she felt guilty.

She had violated her "should" and had given in to her "want." My heart melted, however, and I called her name again. Sensing forgiveness, Tina darted into my hands. (I always was a softy.)

Now, I may be overdoing it a bit. I don't know if a dog can really feel guilty or not. But I do know a human can. And whether the sin is as slight as chasing a butterfly or as serious as sleeping with another man's wife, the effects are the same.

Guilt creeps in on cat's paws and steals whatever joy might have flickered in our eyes. Confidence is replaced by doubt, and honesty is elbowed out by rationalization. Exit peace. Enter turmoil. Just as the pleasure of indulgence ceases, the hunger for relief begins.

Our vision is shortsighted and our myopic life now has but one purpose—to find release for our guilt. Or as Paul questioned for all of us, "What a wretched man I am! Who will rescue me from this body of death?"[1]

That's not a new question. One hardly opens the Bible before he encounters humanity coping, or more frequently, failing to cope, with guilt. Adam and Eve's rebellion led to shame and hiding. Cain's jealousy led to murder and banishment. And before long, the entire human race was afflicted. Evil abounded and the people grew wicked. The heart of man grew so cold that he no longer sought relief for his calloused conscience. And, in what has to be the most fearful scripture in the Bible, God says that he was sorry that he had made man on earth.[2]

All of this from man's inability to cope with sin.

If only we had a guilt-kidney that would pass on our failures or a built-in eraser that would help us live with ourselves. But we don't. In fact, that is precisely the problem.

Man cannot cope with guilt alone.

When Adam was created, he was created without the ability to cope with guilt. Why? Because he was not made to make mistakes. But when he did, he had no way to deal with it. When God pursued him to help him, Adam covered his nakedness and hid in shame.

Man by himself cannot deal with his own guilt. He must have help from the outside. In order to forgive himself, he must have forgiveness from the one he nas offended. Yet man is unworthy to ask God for forgiveness.

That, then, is the whole reason for the cross.

The cross did what sacrificed lambs could not do. It erased our sins, not for a year, but for eternity. The cross did what man could not do. It granted us the right to talk with, love, and even live with God.

You can't do that by yourself. I don't care how many worship services you attend or good deeds you do, your goodness is insufficient. You *can't* be good enough to deserve forgiveness. No one bats a thousand. No one bowls three hundred. No one. Not you, not me, not anyone.

That's why we have guilt in the world.

That's why we need a savior.

You can't forgive me for my sins nor can I forgive you for yours. Two kids in a mud puddle can't clean each other. They need someone clean. Someone spotless. We need someone clean too.

That's why we need a savior.

What my little puppy needed was exactly what you and I need—a master who would extend his hands and say, "Come on, that's okay." We don't need a master who will judge us on our performance, or we'll fall woefully short. Trying to make it to heaven on our own goodness is like trying to get to the moon on a moon beam; nice idea, but try it and see what happens.

Listen. Quit trying to quench your own guilt. You can't do it. There's no way. Not with a bottle of whiskey or perfect Sunday School attendance. Sorry. I don't care how bad you are. You can't be bad enough to forget it. And I don't care how good you are. You can't be good enough to overcome it.

You need a Savior.

[1]Romans 7:24
[2]Genesis 6:6

28

GOD'S TESTIMONY

*T*hough the little farm was only two hours away in mileage, it was at least a century away in time.

My friend, Sebastão, had invited me to his hometown of Marecá, a spot-in-the-road town about seventy miles from Rio de Janeiro. He was a twenty-six-year-old factory worker who had visited our congregation and was involved in a Bible study. Slow-talking, tall, gangly; this fellow was no city slicker. He was a bit too honest, simple, and quick to smile to have any roots in the urban jungle.

I welcomed the opportunity to see some of the Brazilian countryside. What I didn't know, however, was that I was about to learn a lesson on faith.

I could feel my neck muscles relax as we left Rio and her polluted war of traffic in the rearview mirror. My little VW sedan leaned in and out of the picturesque roads that wound through the hills. The scenery was not unlike bluegrass Kentucky; thick, rich green grass, generous valleys, friendly hillsides dotted with grazing Herefords.

Soon we pulled off the four-lane onto a two-lane; then, after a half dozen "bear rights" and "stay lefts" we emptied out onto a one-lane dirt road.

"Normally, I come by bus," Sebastão explained. "I usually have to walk this piece." A "piece" it was not. For at least another four miles we stirred up the rarely-driven-upon country dust. In the process we passed a younger fellow leading a mule that carried two churns of milk. "That's my cousin," Sebastão volunteered. "He comes by every morning at sunup with fresh milk." The thin road carried us through a myriad colors; the white-trunked eucalyptus trees sat like candles on a cake of dark green pasture. The Brazilian sky was brilliantly blue and the hills rustic and red.

"Stop here," I was instructed. I pulled to a stop in front of a big wooden gate suspended between two fence posts. "Just a second and I'll open the gate."

If I thought the road we had just taken was small, the one that led us from the gate to the house was invisible. I kept thinking how I needed a jeep as we bounded through the grass, slid under the bushes, crept between the trees, and finally appeared in a clearing next to an old stucco house.

Waiting for us was Sebastão's father, Senhor José. He certainly did not look his seventy plus years. Eyes shaded by an old straw hat, he smiled a toothless grin when he saw us. His barrelled brown chest and narrow waist testified to thousands of hours of hoeing and planting. His flat bare feet were stained the color of the soil and his hands were crusty and thick.

"Good to have you," he welcomed. You could tell he meant it.

The little house made me think of pictures I'd seen of the United States during the Depression. Unlit kerosene lanterns (no electricity). Basins of water to wash up in (no running water). A wall lined with well-worn hoes, shovels, and picks (no modern equipment). The kitchen was a separate hut that sat next to the front door of the house. I was intrigued by the stove. It was made of hard, baked mud, molded in a long narrow piece about four feet long and three feet tall. A four or five inch trough ran down the center to hold the wood. The ever-present pots cooking the beans and rice straddled the hot trough. I felt a long way from Rio.

Senhor José took me on a tour through his segment of the world. For thirty-seven years he had plowed and tilled his two acres. It was obvious that he knew every hole and turn.

"I fed fourteen mouths off this land," he smiled, fingering a lettuce plant. "Where did you say you were from?" "The U.S."

"What do you do here?"

I explained a bit about my work. He did not respond but led me over to a little creek where he sat on a rock and began undressing.

"Gonna take a bath, Pop?" Sebastão asked.

"Yep, it's Saturday."

"Well, we'll see you back at the house then."

Sebastão led me through a sugar cane patch where he cut a stalk, skinned it, and gave me a piece to eat. We made our way back to the house and sat down at the outdoor dinner table. The benches were worn smooth from decades of use.

About that time Senhor José appeared with clean trousers, hat removed, and hair wet.

Though we hadn't talked for half an hour, he renewed the conversation exactly where we had left it (you could tell he'd been thinking).

"A missionary, huh? Your job must be pretty easy."

"How's that?" I asked.

"I have no trouble believing in God. After I see what he has done on my little farm, year after year, it is easy to believe." He smiled another toothless grin and yelled to his wife to bring out some beans.

As we drove home, I couldn't help thinking about Senhor José. My, what a simple life. No traffic jams, airline schedules, or long lines. Far removed from Wall Street, IRS, and mortgages. Unacquainted with Johannine theology, Martin Luther, or Christian evidences.

I thought of his faith, his ability to believe, and his surprise that there were some who couldn't. I compared his faith with others I knew had more difficulty believing; a university student, a wealthy import-export man, an engineer. There was such a difference between José and the others.

His faith was rooted in the simple miracles that he witnessed every day:

A small seed becoming a towering tree.

A thin stalk pushing back the earth.

A rainbow arching in the midst of the thundercloud.

It was easy for him to believe. I can see why. Someone who witnesses God's daily display of majesty doesn't find the secret of Easter absurd. Someone who depends upon the mysteries of nature for his livelihood doesn't find it difficult to depend on an unseen God for his salvation.

"Nature," wrote Jonathan Edwards, "is God's greatest evangelist."

"Faith," wrote Paul, "does not rest in the wisdom of men, but in the power of God."[1]

"God's testimony," wrote David, "makes wise the simple."[2]

God's testimony. When was the last time you witnessed it? A stroll through knee-high grass in a green meadow. An hour listening to seagulls or looking at seashells on the beach. Or witnessing the shafts of sunlight brighten the snow on a crisp winter dawn. Miracles that almost match the magnitude of the empty tomb happen all around us; we only have to pay attention.

The old Brazilian farmer gave me a time-tested principle to take home. He reminded me that there is a certain understanding of God on the cross that comes only with witnessing his daily testimony. There comes a time when we should lay down our pens and commentaries and step out of our offices and libraries. To really understand and believe in the miracle on the cross, we'd do well to witness God's miracles every day.

[1] 1 Corinthians 2:5, author's paraphrase
[2] Psalms 19

29

DYNAMITE DECISIONS

I still chuckle when I think about the joke I heard about the game warden who got a quick lesson on fishing.

It seems he noticed how this one particular fellow named Sam consistently caught more fish than anyone else. Whereas the other guys would only catch three or four a day, Sam would come in off the lake with a boat full. Stringer after stringer was always packed with freshly caught trout.

The warden, curious, asked Sam his secret. The successful fisherman invited the game warden to accompany him and observe. So the next morning the two met at the dock and took off in Sam's boat. When they got to the middle of the lake, they stopped the boat and the warden sat back to see how it was done.

Sam's approach was simple. He took out a stick of dynamite, lit it, and threw it in the air. The explosion rocked the lake with such a force that dead fish immediately began to surface. Sam took out a net and started scooping them up.

Well, you can imagine the reaction of the game warden. When he recovered from the shock of it all, he began yelling at Sam. "You can't do this! I'll put you in jail, buddy! You will be paying every fine there is in the book!" Sam, meanwhile, set his net down and took out another stick of dynamite. He lit it and tossed it in the lap of the game warden with these words, "Are you going to sit there all day complaining or are you going to fish?"

The poor warden was left with a fast decision to make. He was yanked, in one second, from an observer to a participant. A dynamite of a choice had to be made and be made quickly!

Life is like that. Few days go by without our coming face to face with an uninvited, unanticipated, yet unavoidable decision. Like a crashing snow bank, these decisions tumble upon us without warning. They disorientate and bewilder. Quick. Immediate. Sudden. No council, no study, no advice. Pow! All of a sudden you are hurled into the air of uncertainty and only instinct will determine if you will land on your feet.

Want a good example? Look at the three apostles in the garden. Sound asleep. Weary from a full meal and a full week, their eyelids too heavy, they are awakened by Jesus only to tumble back into dreamland. The last time, however, they were awakened by Jesus to clanging swords, bright torches, and loud voices.

"There he is!"

"Let's get him!"

A shout. A kiss. A shuffling of feet. A slight skirmish. All of a sudden it is decision time. No time to huddle. No time to pray. No time to meditate or consult friends. Decision.

Peter makes his. Out comes the sword. Off goes the ear. Jesus rebukes him. Now what?

Mark, who apparently was a young eyewitness, wrote these words, "Then everyone deserted him and fled."[1]

That's a nice way of saying they ran like scared mice. All of them? All of them. Even Peter? Yes, even Peter. James? Yes, James. John? John, his beloved one? Yes, John ran away too. They all did. The decision came upon them like a halloween ghost and they ran fast. The only thing that was moving faster than their feet was their pulse rate. All those words of loyalty and commitment were left behind in a cloud of dust.

But before we get too hard on these quick-footed followers, let's look at ourselves. Maybe you have been in the garden of decision a few times yourself. Has your loyalty ever been challenged? Have you ever passed by this trap door of the devil?

For the teenager it could be a joint being passed around the circle. For the business man it could be an offer to make a little cash "under the table." For the wife it could be a chance for her to give her "two bits" of juicy gossip. For the student it could be an opportunity to improve his grade while looking at his friend's quiz. For the husband it could mean an urge to lose his temper over his wife's spending. One minute we are in a calm boat on a lake talking about fishing, in the next we have a stick of dynamite in our hands.

More often than not, the end result is catastrophe. Rather than calmly defusing the bomb, we let it explode. We find ourselves doing the very thing we detest. The child in us lunges forward, uncontrolled and unrestrained, and the adult in us follows behind shaking his head.

Now, it doesn't have to be like that. Jesus didn't panic. He, too, heard the swords and saw the clubs, but he didn't lose his head. And it was his head that the Romans wanted!

In rereading the garden scene we can see why. One statement made by our master offers two basic tools for keeping our cool in the heat of a decision. "Watch and pray so that you will not fall into temptation."[2]

The first tool: "Watch." They don't come any more practical than that. Watch. Stay alert. Keep your eyes open. When you see sin coming, duck. When you anticipate an awkward encounter, turn around. When you sense temptation, go the other way.

All Jesus is saying is, "Pay attention." You know your weaknesses. You also know the situations in which your weaknesses are most vulnerable. *Stay out of those situations*. Back seats. Late hours. Night clubs. Poker games. Bridge parties. Movie theaters. Whatever it is that gives Satan a foothold in your life, stay away from it. Watch out!

Second tool: "Pray." Prayer isn't telling God anything new. There is not a sinner nor a saint who would surprise him. What prayer does is invite God to walk the shadowy pathways of life with us. Prayer is asking God to watch ahead for falling trees and tumbling boulders and to bring up the rear, guarding our backside from the poison darts of the devil.

"Watch and pray." Good advice. Let's take it. It could be the difference between a peaceful day on the lake and a stick of dynamite blowing up in our faces.

[1]Mark 14:50
[2]Mark 14:38

30

WHAT DID YOU EXPECT?

My first rub with expectations came when I was a red-headed, freckle-faced fourth grader. It all had to do with my first girlfriend, Marlene. Man, was I high on Marlene! She was the Queen's queen. She could turn my head and accelerate my pulse rate like no one else. She must have been part hypnotist, because when I was with her all I could do was grin. Stare and grin. No words. No dialogue. Just a gawking, drooling ten-year-old "in love."

Then one day she consented to "go with me" (or, in adult terms, be my girlfriend). Wow! Fireworks, music, stars. Strike up the band. "I'm yours, your Highness."

There was only one problem. I'd never had a girlfriend before. Maybe that's why a well-meaning friend gave me some advice during recess one day. "A boyfriend is supposed to do things for his girl."

"Like what?"

"Like walk her to class, dummy! Sit with her at the lunch table. That kind of stuff."

So that day at lunch, I waited at the cafeteria door for her to arrive. When she appeared, I gentlemanly took her books, extended my arm, and walked her to the lunch line.

All was fine and good until the next day after school. Her best friend came up to me and broke the news, "Marlene wants to break up." I was dumbfounded. "What for?" "Because you didn't sit with her at lunch today."

What had I done?

I had my first questions about women that day. I would later learn, however, that the problem was not a female problem; it was and is a human problem.

It is the problem of expectations. You see, Marlene now had certain expectations of me. I sat with her at lunch one day, therefore I should sit with her at lunch every day. Though nothing was ever stated, the perception was there. Though no agreement was ever made, the assumption was just as strong. She *expected* me to be there. I let her down. (We broke up.)

Sound familiar? How about your experience with expectations? They can get serious, you know. They've been known to do a lot more than just mess up a fourth grade romance. Divorce, job tension, poor self-image, family dissension, world wars, embittered friendships—all these can be caused by this same little culprit, expectations.

Expectations are like rifles. Used correctly and appropriately, they are valuable and necessary. But, oh, how quickly are they misused. How quickly do we load their chambers, cock their triggers, and draw a bead on those we love. Quietly we pull the trigger. "You let me down." And we both fall victim to the bullet of expectation.

Ever caught yourself using these tell-tale words of unhealthy expectations? How about with your children?

"Now, your big brother made an 'A' in chemistry, and we know you'll do just as well."

"When I was your age, son, I made the *varsity* football team."

"Are you going to be a smart doctor just like your Dad?"

"Now, honey, don't even think about *that* university. When you graduate you're going to our alma mater. I'm already saving for your tuition!"

Or maybe these with your spouse:

"If you had a better salary, John, we could afford that house."

"Honey, I promised Paul I'd play golf next Saturday. You don't mind, do you?"

"It's not my fault that the kitchen is a mess. It's the wife's job to keep the house."

Or, at work:

"Eric, I've got high hopes for you in this company. Don't let me down."

"I know it's after 5:00 p.m. But I thought you wouldn't mind if we saw one more client."

"I know you haven't had a vacation, Phil. But those who really care about this firm are willing to sacrifice."

Expectations. They create conditional love. "I love you, but I'll love you even more *if*. . ."

Now, I know what you're thinking. Shouldn't we expect the best out of each other? Shouldn't we encourage each other to strive for excellence and never settle for anything else?

Absolutely.

But it was Christ on the cross who taught us how to use expectations. Does he demand a lot? You better believe it. Does he expect much? Only our best. Does he have expectations? Just that we leave everything, deny all, and follow him.

The difference? Jesus couched his expectations with two important companions. Forgiveness and acceptance.

Study attentively these words written by Paul: "While we were still sinners, Christ died for us."[1]

When did he die for us? When we reached perfection? No. When we overcame all temptation? Hardly. When we mastered the Christian walk? Far from it. Christ died when we were still sinners. His sacrifice, then, was not dependent on our performance.

When we love with expectations, we say, "I love you. But I'll love you even more if . . ."

Christ's love had none of this. No strings, no expectations, no hidden agendas, no secrets. His love for us was, and is, up front and clear. "I love you," he says. "Even if you let me down. I love you in spite of your failures."

One step behind the expectations of Christ come his forgiveness and tenderness. Tumble off the tightrope of what our Master expects and you land safely in his net of tolerance.

Expectations. Alone, they are bullets that can kill; but buffered by acceptance and forgiveness, they can bring out the best. Even in teenage romances.

[1]Romans 5:8

31

COME HOME

*T*he practice of using earthly happenings to clarify heavenly truths is no easy task. Yet, occasionally, one comes across a story, legend, or fable that conveys a message as accurately as a hundred sermons and with ten times the creativity. Such is the case with the reading below. I heard it first told by a Brazilian preacher in São Paulo. And though I've shared it countless times, with each telling I am newly warmed and reassured by its message.

The small house was simple but adequate. It consisted of one large room on a dusty street. Its red-tiled roof was one of many in this poor neighborhood on the outskirts of the Brazilian village. It was a comfortable home. Maria and her daughter, Christina, had done what they could to add color to the gray walls and warmth to the hard dirt floor: an old calendar, a faded photograph of a relative, a wooden crucifix. The furnishings were modest: a pallet on either side of the room, a washbasin, and a wood-burning stove.

Maria's husband had died when Christina was an infant. The young mother, stubbornly refusing opportunities to remarry, got a job and set out to raise her young daughter. And now, fifteen years later, the worst years were over. Though Maria's salary as a maid afforded few luxuries, it was reliable and it did provide food and clothes. And now Christina was old enough to get a job to help out.

Some said Christina got her independence from her mother. She recoiled at the traditional idea of marrying young and raising a family. Not that she couldn't have had her pick of husbands. Her olive skin and brown eyes kept a steady stream of prospects at her door. She had an infectious way of throwing her head back and filling the room with laughter. She also had that rare magic some women have that makes every man feel like a king just by being near them. But it was her spirited curiosity that made her keep all the men at arm's length.

She spoke often of going to the city. She dreamed of trading her dusty neighborhood for exciting avenues and city life. Just the thought of this horrified her mother. Maria was always quick to remind Christina of the harshness of the streets. "People don't know you there. Jobs are scarce and the life is cruel. And besides, if you went there, what would you do for a living?"

Maria knew exactly what Christina would do, or would *have* to do for a living. That's why her heart broke when she awoke one morning to find her daughter's bed empty. Maria knew immediately where her daughter had gone. She also knew immediately what she must do to find her. She quickly threw some clothes in a bag, gathered up all her money, and ran out of the house.

On her way to the bus stop she entered a drugstore to get one last thing. Pictures. She sat in the photograph booth, closed the curtain, and spent all she could on pictures of herself. With her purse full of small black-and-white photos, she boarded the next bus to Rio de Janeiro.

Maria knew Christina had no way of earning money. She also knew that her daughter was too stubborn to give up. When pride meets hunger, a human will do things that were before unthinkable. Knowing this, Maria began her search. Bars, hotels, nightclubs, any place with the reputation for street walkers or prostitutes. She went to them all. And at each place she left her picture—taped on a bathroom mirror, tacked to a hotel bulletin board, fastened to a corner phone booth. And on the back of each photo she wrote a note.

It wasn't too long before both the money and the pictures ran out, and Maria had to go home. The weary mother wept as the bus began its long journey back to her small village.

It was a few weeks later that young Christina descended the hotel stairs. Her young face was tired. Her brown eyes no longer danced with youth but spoke of pain and fear. Her laughter was broken. Her dream had become a nightmare. A thousand times over she had longed to trade these countless beds for her secure pallet. Yet the little village was, in too many ways, too far away.

As she reached the bottom of the stairs, her eyes noticed a familiar face. She looked again, and there on the lobby mirror was a small picture of her mother. Christina's eyes burned and her throat tightened as she walked across the room and removed the small photo. Written on the back was this compelling invitation. "Whatever you have done, whatever you have become, it doesn't matter. Please come home."

She did.

"The Son is the radiance of God's glory and the exact representation of his being. . . . "[1]

"Come to me, all you who are weary and burdened, and I will give you rest."[2]

[1]Hebrews 1:3
[2]Matthew 11:28

32

CONSISTENT INCONSISTENCIES

I suspect that the most consistent thing about life has to be its inconsistency.

Choosing not to be neatly categorized, life has opted to be a tossed salad of tragedies and triumphs, profanity and purity, despair and hope. The bad is perplexingly close to the good. The just is frighteningly near to the unfair. And life? Life is always a clock's tick away from death. And evil? Evil is paradoxically close to goodness. It is as if only a sheer curtain separates the two. Given the right lure, at the right moment, aimed at the right weakness, there is not a person alive who wouldn't pull back his curtain and live out his vilest fantasy.

The inconsistency of life.

As a result, one moment can simultaneously usher in sweet victory and crushing defeat. The same day can bring both reunion and separation. The same birth can bring both pain and peace. Truth and half-truth often ride in the same saddle. (And yes, James, good and evil *can* come out of the same mouth.)

"If life was just simpler!" we reason, "More predictable!" But it isn't. Even for the best among us, life is like a wild roller coaster ride of hairpin curves and diving dips.

Maybe that is why there is within all of us just a bit of paranoia, an unsettling insecurity. Oh, we may submerge it some with pin-striped shirts and martinis, but the anxiety of the future is still present. Don't all of us live with a fear of the unknown? Don't all of us dread the horrible day when the thin curtain that separates us from evil might be pulled back and in we would tumble? Cancer. Murder. Rape. Death. How haunting is that gnawing awareness that we are not immune to life's mishaps and perils.

It's this eerie inconsistency that keeps all of us, to one degree or another, living our lives on the edge of our chairs.

Yet, it was in this inconsistency that God had his finest hour. Never did the obscene come so close to the holy as it did on Calvary. Never did the good in the world so tightly intertwine with the bad as it did on the cross. Never did what is right involve itself so intimately with what is wrong, as it did when Jesus was suspended between heaven and earth.

God on a cross. Humanity at its worst. Divinity at its best.

Something is said at the cross about inconsistencies. Something hopeful. Something healing. Simply stated, that which is consistent did battle with that which is inconsistent, and the consistent won.

Something is also said about God himself. God is not stumped by an evil world. He doesn't gasp in amazement at the dearth of our faith or the depth of our failures. We can't surprise God with our cruelties. He knows the condition of the world . . .and loves it just the same. For just when we find a place where God would never be (like on a cross), we look again and there he is, in the flesh.

33

THE ROAR

*T*he door is locked. Deadbolted. Maybe even a chair under the doorknob. Inside sit ten knee-knocking itinerants who are astraddle the fence between faith and fear.

As you look around the room, you wouldn't take them for a bunch who are about to put the kettle of history on high boil. Uneducated. Confused. Calloused hands. Heavy accents. Few social graces. Limited knowledge of the world. No money. Undefined leadership. And on and on.

No, as you look at this motley crew, you wouldn't wager too many paychecks on their future. But something happens to a man when he witnesses someone who has risen from the dead. Something stirs within the soul of a man who has stood within inches of God. Something stirs that is hotter than gold fever and more permanent than passion.

It all started with ten stammering, stuttering men. Though the door was locked, he still stood in their midst. "As the Father has sent me, I am sending you."[1]

And send them he did. Ports. Courtyards. Boats. Synagogues. Prisons. Palaces. They went everywhere.

Their message of the Nazarene dominoed across the civilized world. They were an infectious fever. They were a moving organism. They refused to be stopped. Uneducated drifters who shook history like a housewife shakes a rug.

My, wouldn't it be great to see it happen again?

Many say it's impossible. The world is too hard. Too secular. Too post-Christian. "This is the age of information, not regeneration." So we deadbolt the door for fear of the world.

And as a result, the world goes largely untouched and untaught. Over half of the world has yet to hear the story of the Messiah, much less study it. The few believers who do go out often come home weary and wounded, numbed at the odds and frustrated at the needs.

What would it take to light the fire again? Somehow, those fellows in the upper room did it. They did it without dragging their feet or making excuses. For them it was rather obvious. "All I know is that he was dead and now he is alive."

Something happens to a man when he stands within inches of the Judaean Lion. Something happens when he hears the roar, when he touches the golden mane. Something happens when he gets so close he can feel the Lion's breath. Maybe we could all use a return visit. Maybe we all need to witness his majesty and sigh at his victory. Maybe we need to hear our own commission again. "Will you tell them?" Jesus challenged. "Will you tell them that I came back . . . and that I am coming back again?"

"We will," they nodded. And they did.

Will you?

[1]John 20:21.

STUDY GUIDE

Chapter 1: Final Words, Final Acts

1. *Final words. Final acts. Each one is a window through which the cross can be better understood. Each one opens a treasury of promises.*

A. Why are the final words and actions of a dying person significant? Why are the final words and actions of Christ particularly significant?

B. In preparation for this study read Luke's account of the betrayal, the Last Supper, Jesus' arrest and trial, and his crucifixion in chapters 22 and 23. What things surprise you? What things are hard to comprehend? Considering that these are Jesus' final hours on earth, what one word best depicts his words and actions during these hours?

C. What do you hope to gain from this study of Christ's last words and actions? What will make the difference in how well you succeed? Write down five specific goals for the study, and at the end of the study assess to what extent you have achieved them.

2. *It's much easier to die like Jesus if you have lived like him for a lifetime.*

A. From your observation, to what extent does someone's personality change as he or she gets older? To what extent does a person's character change?

B. What do the following passages reveal about our ability to be like Jesus: 1 Corinthians 2:16; John 14:5-24? What does it mean to have the mind of Christ? What outward indications will there be when we truly live in a Christ-like manner? What does Jesus promise us when we live in a Christ-like manner?

C. What specific character trait would you want to be remembered for at your death? To what extent is that true of you now? What could you do to strengthen that characteristic in yourself?

Chapter 2: Words that Wound

1. *Sometimes I wonder if we don't see Christ's love as much in the people he tolerated as in the pain he endured.*

A. What kinds of "wounds" hurt the most? Physical abuse? Insults? Rejection? Apathy? Prejudice? Revenge? Are there others you would add to the list? Which would you rank as the most difficult to forgive? Why?

B. Which of these wounds did Jesus experience? Give an example of each that he experienced.

C. Read Luke's account of the crucifixion again (Luke 23:26-43), focusing on what was said to Jesus. Would you agree with Max's statement above? Why or why not?

D. If Max's statement is true, in what way might we today cause Jesus more pain than his crucifixion did?

2. *If ever a person deserved a shot at revenge, Jesus did. But he didn't take it. Instead he died for them.*

A. The cliche says "revenge is sweet." How would you describe revenge? Describe a time in which you took revenge. How did you feel afterwards?

B. What do the following passages teach about revenge: Romans 12:17-21; 1 Peter 3:9-17; Ezekiel 25:15-17? How are we to overcome our desire for revenge? When a person responds to injury with kindness, what benefits does it bring? What action does God take in such situations?

C. Why does revenge hurt the one who seeks it more than the one who is the intended recipient? Describe a time in which you overcame a desire for revenge. How did it make you feel? What benefits did it bring?

Chapter 3: Vigilante Vengeance

1. *Anger. It's a peculiar yet predictable emotion. It begins as a drop of water....Yet, get enough of these seemingly innocent drops of anger and before long you've got a bucket full of rage....We become walking time bombs that, given just the right tension and fear, could explode like Mr. Goetz.*

A. How serious a problem is anger in our society? What recent examples can you give that illustrate the problem? Why do you think people are angry? Do you agree that, given the right tension and fear, we are time bombs waiting to explode?

B. How "serious" a sin is anger, judging by Galatians 5:19-21?

C. According to these passages, what typically accompanies anger: Proverbs 14:17, 29; Ecclesiastes 7:9; James 1:19-20? What would these passages indicate as antidotes to anger? In view of these passages, would you say "counting to ten" has some value?

2. *Uncontrolled anger won't better our world, but sympathetic understanding will. Once we see the world and ourselves for what we are, we can help.*

A. What makes you angry? Have you ever been uncontrollably angry? How does it feel? What helps you control your anger?

B. When Stephen was stoned to death, he uttered a similar statement to Jesus' statement. Read Acts 6:8-15 and 7:54—8:1. What parallels are there between Jesus' nature and Stephen's? How did their words at their death affect those around them?

C. Goetz prepared for a situation that made him angry by carrying a gun. What "weapons" could you arm yourself with so that you would be able to handle a difficult situation with understanding instead of anger?

Chapter 4: The Tale of the Crucified Crook

1. *You are valuable just because you exist. Not because of what you do or what you have done, but simply because you are.*

A. To what extent are people valued in today's culture? What gives a person value, according to today's standards? What affects society's view of the worth of the individual?

B. What do the following passages teach about the value God places upon people: Romans 5:8; Ephesians 2:4-5; Titus 3:4-7; 1 John 4:9-10?

C. Do we behave as if we have intrinsic value? If people truly believed they had intrinsic value, what problems in society would no longer exist?

2. *It makes me smile to think that there is a grinning ex-con walking the golden streets who knows more about grace than a thousand theologians.*

A. What do you think is most significant about the story of the crucified crook?

B. Read Luke 23:32-43. What can you learn about the two criminals from this brief episode? Why do *you* think Jesus gave this criminal a promise of paradise?

C. How do you think the crucified crook would explain grace in one sentence?

Chapter 5: Leaving Is Loving

1. *What kind of God would give you families and then ask you to leave them? What kind of God would give you friends and then ask you to say goodbye?*

A. Do you know someone who has had to choose between family or friends and a commitment to God? What sacrifices were made? What was the result?

B. What do you think Jesus meant in Matthew 19:28-29? In what way do Matthew 6:33 and Matthew 12:46-50 shed light on his meaning?

C. In what way did Jesus live by this principle?

2. *John fastened his arm around Mary a little tighter. Jesus was asking him to be the son that a mother needs and that in some ways he never was.*

A. Considering all the physical and spiritual struggles surrounding the crucifixion, why do you think this personal story about Jesus' mother was recorded for us?

B. Read John 19:25-27. How does this event indicate Jesus' love for his family? What does it indicate about his relationship with his friends? How do you reconcile his love for his family and friends with his statement in Matthew 19:28-29?

C. What did Paul say in 1 Timothy 5:8 about caring for one's family? How would you explain the balance in our responsibility to our family and to our faith?

Chapter 6: The Cry of Loneliness

1. *I'm writing to those of you who can find a lonely person simply by looking in the mirror.*

A. How would you describe loneliness? When are people most susceptible to loneliness? What antidotes to loneliness do we use?

B. Read Psalm 139:1-18 and Acts 17:24-28. In what way do they offer comfort to someone who feels lonely?

C. Are there people you know who are lonely? Which groups within the church are particularly vulnerable—those who have lost loved ones, the elderly, those who are away from their family and friends, missionaries supported by your church? Are there others? In what specific ways could you help dispel their loneliness?

2. *And although he may offer no answer, although he may solve no dilemma, although the question may freeze painfully in mid-air, he who also was once alone, understands.*

A. Why was it important for Jesus to be totally separated from God for a time?

B. Do you agree with Max's interpretation of this haunting passage (Matthew 27:46)? How do you understand the word "forsaken" in this passage? Of all the statements at the cross, in what way is this the most heartrending? Read Psalm 22. In what way does David's anguish parallel Jesus' anguish?

C. Can you imagine any greater pain and loneliness than Jesus suffered? How does it affect you to know that he chose to suffer that for your sake?

Chapter 7: I Thirst

1. *Just at the right time we are reminded that the one to whom we pray knows our feelings. He knows temptation. He has felt discouraged.*

A. Why is it important to realize not only the divinity of Jesus, but also his humanity?

B. According to Hebrews 2:14-18 and Hebrews 4:14-16, in what ways can Jesus identify with us as humans? What blessings does that bring to us? How does Jesus now act on our behalf?

C. In prayer, how do you balance reverence for Jesus as God and creator of the universe with the awareness that Jesus shared in our humanity and understands our weaknesses?

2. *We are most indebted to John for choosing to include verse 28 of chapter 19. It reads simply: "I'm thirsty."*

A. Why does this verse seem out of character with Jesus' other statements at the cross? What significance does it have for us?

B. Read John 19:28-29. Why did Jesus say, "I am thirsty"? Read Psalm 69:21 and Psalm 22. What parallels are there between these psalms and the events of the crucifixion?

C. How would you describe the intensity of Jesus' thirst on the cross? In Matthew 5:6, Jesus said we also should be thirsty. When were you most intensely thirsty? If you now had the same craving for righteousness as you then had for water, how would it change your life?

Chapter 8: Creative Compassion

1. *The ultimate act of creative compassion is revealed. God on a cross. The Creator being sacrificed for the creation. God convincing man once and for all that forgiveness still follows failure.*

A. What does Max mean by calling the crucifixion the "ultimate act of creative compassion"?

B. In what way was the crucifixion of Christ the result of mankind's greatest failure? Has there ever been a greater need for forgiveness than for killing the Son of God? Based on the following passages, how would you describe God's forgiving nature: 1 John 1:7-9; Luke 6:37-38; Acts 10:42-43; Psalm 103:1-5; Acts 3:19? What is required of those seeking forgiveness?

C. How would you assure someone about God's ability to forgive any sin?

2. *"It is finished." The mission was finished. All that the master painter needed to do was done and was done in splendor.*

A. What is your mission in life? In what ways are you in the process of accomplishing it? At what point would your mission be finished?

B. Read John 19:28-30. What did Jesus mean by "It is finished"? What was finished? What tasks had not been completed? How does his statement clarify his mission?

C. Spend some time writing down a personal mission statement. Then make a list of your priorities based on your mission statement. What changes do you want to make in view of your mission and priorities?

Chapter 9: It Is Finished

1. *Jesus didn't quit. But don't think for one minute that he wasn't tempted to.*

A. Do you think Jesus seriously considered not dying on the cross? What do you think would have been the strongest temptation for not going through with it?

B. In the following passages, what could have tempted Jesus to give up: Mark 10:32-45; Mark 14:32-42; Mark 9:33-41?

C. What did Jesus do to gain the strength to continue? What are our greatest sources of strength when we are tempted to give up?

2. *God didn't call us to be successful, just faithful.*

A. Do you agree with this statement? How would you distinguish between being successful and being faithful? Can you be successful without being faithful? Can you be faithful without being successful? Explain.

B. What do the following passages teach about faithfulness: Matthew 24:12-13; Romans 2:6-7; Colossians 1:22-23; Hebrews 12:1-12? What will characterize the person who remains faithful? Why is the analogy of the runner an apt comparison for the Christian life?

C. To what extent do we value faithfulness in our society—faithfulness to our word, to our mates, to our responsibilities, to our God? To what extent does our culture value success? How can you model greater faithfulness for those around you?

Chapter 10: Take Me Home

1. *The two are again one. The abandoned is now found. The schism is now bridged.*

A. How would you describe the unity of God and Christ? What earthly comparisons could you make?

B. According to these passages, how did Jesus describe his unity with God the Father: John 10:38; John 14:10-11; John 17:20-21? What was so significant about Jesus being reunited with God?

C. At what times do you feel the greatest sense of oneness with Jesus? According to John 17:20-26, what results from a unity with Jesus?

2. *Satan's vultures have been scattered. Hell's demons have been jailed. Death has been damned.*

A. In what way was the moment of Satan's apparent greatest triumph actually the moment of his greatest defeat?

B. Read John 12:31-33; John 14:28-31; John 16:5-11; and Hebrews 2:14-16. What do they teach about the impact of Jesus' death on the power of Satan?

C. Even though Jesus defeated Satan, in what ways do we continue to allow him to have power? According to these passages, how does he attempt to destroy our relationship with God: 2 Corinthians 11:3-4, 13-15; 1 Peter 5:8-9; John 8:42-47?

Chapter 11: Who Would Have Believed?

1. There was something about the crucifixion that made every witness either step toward it or away from it. It simultaneously compelled and repelled.

A. Of the witnesses of the crucifixion, with whom do you best identify? Why?

B. Look at some of the people who were repelled by it: Judas (Luke 22:1-6); Herod, the chief priests, the Sanhedrin, and the crowds (Luke 23:1-25). What caused them to reject Jesus' claim to be the Messiah? Which of their reasons for rejecting Jesus are still prevalent today?

C. Look at some of the people who were compelled by it: Joseph of Arimathea and Nicodemus (John 19:38-42); the women at the cross (John 19:25-27); the "crucified crook" (Luke 23:39-43). What lessons can we learn from their examples?

2. We can do what we want with the cross. We can examine its history. We can study its theology. We can reflect upon its prophecies. Yet the one thing we can't do is walk away in neutral.

A. How do you respond to people who say that Jesus was merely a good man, not the Son of God? If Jesus had not been the Son of God, why would it not be accurate to say he was a good man?

B. In 1 Corinthians 15:1-20, what arguments does Paul present about the significance of Christ's resurrection from the dead? If a person doesn't accept that, what is left?

C. In what way do these Old Testament passages serve as Messianic prophecies: Micah 5:1-5; Isaiah 11; Zechariah 9:9?

D. What causes you to believe that Jesus is the Son of God? Is there one thing in particular, or is it an accumulation of evidence? Are you willing to bet your eternal destiny on the fact that Jesus is who he says he is?

Chapter 12: Faces in the Crowd

1. *Some believe that Malchus was later numbered among the believers at Jerusalem. We don't know for sure.*

A. If you had been given the opportunity to interview Malchus after this scene in the garden, what questions would you have asked him? What do you think happened to Malchus? Why?

B. Read the story of Malchus in John 18:1-11, Matthew 26:47-56, Mark 14:43-52, and Luke 22:47-53. What information is unique to each account? What insights into Jesus does this incident give us?

C. What contemporary example do you know of someone who has been "touched" by Jesus with dramatic results? Is Jesus' power to change lives today any less miraculous than his healing of Malchus? What benefit is there in telling the story of Malchus or the story of someone today who is changed by Jesus?

2. *Ironic as it may appear, one of the hardest things to do is to be saved by grace.*

A. Do you agree with Max's statement? If so, do you agree with his explanation that pride gets in the way? How does pride hinder us? For what other reasons might people reject grace?

B. What do the following passages indicate about our ability to earn our salvation: Romans 4:4-8, 13-16; Ephesians 2:8-10; John 1:12-13; Romans 11:5-6? Why is it difficult to accept salvation as a gift from God?

C. What wisdom does Proverbs offer on the subject of pride in the following verses: 11:2; 16:18-20; 29:23? According to these verses, what is the opposite of pride in ourselves? How does that fit with the concept of grace?

Chapter 13: Well ... Almost

1. *It's one thing to forgive yourself for something you did. It is something else to try to forgive yourself for something that you might have done, but didn't.*

A. Recount a time when you regretted not doing something, perhaps a missed opportunity to help someone, a relationship you let grow apart, or a time when you didn't stand up for your faith. What held you back? Do you have lingering regrets about your lack of action?

B. How seriously does God take our inaction? What indications are given in these examples: Matthew 25:14-30 and Matthew 25:31-46? Are there any more serious warnings in Scripture than these?

C. From what you see in the above passages, what expectations does God have of you?

2. *No, Jesus never had room for "almost" and he still doesn't. "Almost" may count in horseshoes and hand grenades, but with the Master, it is just as good as a "never."*

A. Max says Jesus demands absolute obedience. How do we view "absolutes"—absolute trust, absolute truth, absolute commitment? To what are we willing to dedicate ourselves absolutely? Has "absolute" become obsolete?

B. How do Mark 10:17-31 and Matthew 25:1-13 support Max's statement that "almost" is as good as "never"? How would you summarize the message of each account?

C. How would you answer a non-Christian friend who said that Jesus' demand for absolute obedience was unfair or unrealistic?

Chapter 14: The Ten Who Ran

1. *I haven't met a person yet who hasn't done the very thing he swore he would never do. We've all walked the streets of Jerusalem.*

A. What are some of the things you thought you would never do—only to find yourself doing them? Perhaps it is a parenting style you thought you would never use with your kids. Perhaps it is a sin you never thought you would be guilty of. Perhaps it is the very thing you dislike in others. Why do we do the very things we want not to do?

B. How did Paul describe this same problem in Romans 7:14-25? What caused him to be at war with himself? How did he understand the struggle? What was his salvation?

C. Are you sensing any spiritual struggles right now? What could you do to "arm" the "slave to God's law"? What could you do to "disarm" the "slave to the law of sin"?

2. *He who forgave his followers stands ready to forgive the rest of us. All we have to do is come back.*

A. The apostles had seen the miracles, had listened to the teachings, and had heard Jesus foretell his death. Why did they not understand? Why did they run?

B. We often refer to the apostle Thomas as "doubting Thomas," yet what do we learn about his faith in John 11:1-16? Like the others, Thomas left behind his faith in Jesus, at least for a time. Read John 20:19-31. How did Jesus make a special point of assuring Thomas? What reassurance does Jesus give us?

C. Luke 15:11-32 gives one of the most poignant portrayals of God's willingness to take us back if we will just come home. Read this account, putting God's name in the place of the father and your name in the place of the younger son.

Chapter 15: The One Who Stayed

1. *One gets the impression that to John, Jesus was above all a loyal companion.*

A. Why do you think John refers to himself as the "disciple whom Jesus loved"? Did Jesus love John more than the other disciples?

B. Notice some of the special occasions that John shared with Jesus: Luke 9:28-36; John 13:18-27; Matthew 26:36-37; John 19:25-27. What would indicate that Jesus relied on him in particular?

C. The Gospel of John is quite different from the other gospel accounts. For one thing, John likes to record discourses of Jesus with one person at a time, such as Jesus' conversations with Nicodemus, the woman at the well, and the royal official. Devote a week to reading the Gospel of John. As the disciple perhaps closest to Jesus, does John give a more person-centered account of the events? What other insights do you gain from his unique perspective?

2. *John teaches us that the strongest relationship with Christ may not necessarily be a complicated one.*

A. Of the people you know, who would you say has the strongest relationship with Christ? How would you describe that relationship? Has it come from formal training, family training, life experiences, or personal study?

B. How did John describe the essence of relationship with Jesus in the following passages: John 14:21; 14:23; 16:27?

C. What will be the natural outgrowth of our love for Jesus according to John 15:9-17?

D. How would you condense John's message on relationship with Jesus into one sentence?

Chapter 16: The Hill of Regret

1. *While Jesus was climbing up the hill of Calvary, Judas was climbing another hill; the hill of regret.*

A. How do you view the character of Judas? How could he spend all that time with Jesus and then betray him? Why did he so quickly regret his decision?

B. Read the following accounts of Judas in John 12:4-6; Matthew 26:14-16; John 13:2; Matthew 26:17-30; and John 13:18-30. What insights do they give into Judas?

C. Read Matthew's account of Judas's regret in Matthew 27:1-10. What further insight does it give into the character of Judas?

D. In what way are the traits of Judas common to all of us to one degree or another?

2. *It takes just as much faith to believe that Jesus can look past my betrayals as it does to believe that he rose from the dead. Both are just as miraculous.*

A. What is the very first thing that comes to mind when you think of Jesus' miracles? Something in biblical times or something in the present? Do we tend to view any present-day occurrence as having the significance of Jesus' miracles while he was on earth? Is Jesus an active or passive participant in your life?

B. What assurances do the following passages provide about God's willingness to forgive even those who betrayed his son: Acts 2:22-47; James 4:7-10; 1 John 1:9? What blessings accompany forgiveness from God?

C. How would you counsel someone struggling to forgive himself for his sins? What verses would you direct him to?

Chapter 17: The Gospel of the Second Chance

1. *No wonder they call it the gospel of the second chance.*

A. What is meant by the "gospel of the second chance"? What other names could it be given?

B. Of all the followers who deserted Jesus, perhaps Peter's story is the most striking. Read the account of his denial of Jesus in Mark 14:27-31, 66-72 and then the angel's response after Jesus' resurrection in Mark 16:1-7. Also read Luke 24:33-34 and John 21:15-19. What message is conveyed in Peter's being singled out? What seems to be Jesus' attitude toward Peter—frustration, disappointment, concern, love?

C. On what other occasions had Peter been given a second chance? Read Matthew 14:22-33 and 17:1-8. In what way did Jesus give him additional chances? What appears to be Jesus' attitude toward Peter on each occasion?

D. What do you think is Jesus' attitude about giving you a second chance, or a third chance, or a fourth? Would he do any less for you than for Peter?

2. *It's not every day that you find someone who will give you a second chance—much less someone who will give you a second chance every day.*

A. Can you think of a time you were given a second chance? How did it affect you? How willing are you to offer others a second chance?

B. What does Matthew 18:21-35 say about second chances? What does Psalm 78 say about God's willingness to provide second chances? How many instances of a second chance does the psalm record? What does Job 33:12-30 teach about God's active role in second chances?

C. As a reminder that he is the God of second chances, write out Lamentations 3:19-26 and place it where you can read it every morning.

Chapter 18: Leave Room for the Magic

1. *We make the same mistake that Thomas made: we forget that "impossible" is one of God's favorite words.*

A. What "impossibilities" had Thomas witnessed? Why do you think he doubted that Jesus had risen from the dead?

B. What assurance does Ephesians 3:20 give us that God is still in the "impossible" business? Is this verse true for believers today as it was for the original recipients of the letter? What is "his power that is at work within us"?

C. What goal has seemed too impossible for even God to fulfill? What could you begin specifically praying for in order to reach that goal? What additional steps could you begin taking toward the goal?

2. *Anytime you mix loyalty with a little imagination, you've got a man of God on your hands.*

A. Do you know some people who, like Thomas, exemplify a mixture of loyalty and imagination in serving God? Give an example. What makes them effective servants?

B. Look at these examples of people who were loyal and imaginative in serving God: Abigail (1 Samuel 25:1-35); Moses' mother (Exodus 1:22—2:10); and the friends of the paralytic (Mark 2:1-12). How was each loyal to God? How was each imaginative? What good resulted in each case?

C. How would you rate your "loyalty quotient"? How would you rate your "imagination quotient"? What cues could you take from Thomas and the others about how to increase both?

Chapter 19: A Candle in the Cavern

1. *Jesus had no room for those who specialized in making religion a warlord, and faith a footrace. No room at all.*

A. With whom was Jesus most patient during his time on earth? With whom was he least tolerant? Whom do you think Jesus would be least tolerant of if he had been born into our world today?

B. Read Matthew 23. Whom is he talking about in this chapter? What was their role in Jewish society? Make a list of the practices for which he condemns them.

C. To what extent do each of those problems exist in religion today?

2. *And it is still often the case that one has to find faith in spite of the church instead of in the church.*

A. To what extent would you agree with Max's statement? Why do you think it is true, or not true?

B. Notice some of the people Jesus praised for their faith: the Roman centurion (Luke 7:1-10); the Canaanite woman (Matthew 15:21-28 and Mark 7:24-30); and, as is implied by Jesus' actions, the thief on the cross (Luke 23:39-43). In each case, how was faith found in an unexpected place?

C. What lesson is there for us in these examples? Do we ignore people that we consider unlikely candidates for faith in Jesus? Where could you invest greater efforts in the future?

Chapter 20: Miniature Messengers

1. *It's not just tears that are the issue, it's what they represent. They represent the heart, the spirit, and the soul of a person. To put a lock and key on your emotions is to bury part of your Christ-likeness!*

A. How comfortable are we with showing our emotions? Why are we reluctant to publicly display our emotions? To what extent do we attribute a show of emotion to gender or personality type as opposed to being a natural and necessary part of every person?

B. What emotions does Christ reveal in these passages: the death of Lazarus (John 11:17-36); seeing Jerusalem (Luke 19:41-44); on the Mount of Olives (Luke 22:39-46)?

C. What physical price do we pay when we bottle up our emotions? What spiritual price do we pay when we suppress our emotions?

2. *You can't go to the cross with just your head and not your heart.*

A. Do you agree with Max's statement? What is the danger in having a religion that is totally heart and no head? What is the danger in having a religion that is totally head and no heart?

B. What emotions were displayed by those who witnessed the death and resurrection of Jesus: the eyewitnesses to the crucifixion (Luke 23:47-49); the people on the road to Emmaus (Luke 24:13-32); those who followed him (Mark 16:9-10; John 20:19-20)?

C. Should our emotions be any different than theirs? How can we prevent becoming jaded by the familiarity of the story?

Chapter 21: Alive

1. In this chapter, it is as if Max captures freeze frames of the events from the Garden of Gethsemane to the resurrection. What is the effect of these quick images?

2. Look at each event. Which word in each paragraph best depicts it?

3. What other words you would add to each event?

4. Read the account of these events, this time from the Gospel of Matthew (26:36—28:10). What other images do you see in Matthew's account?

Chapter 22: Open Arms

1. *The reassuring lesson is clear. God used (and uses!) people to change the world. People! Not saints or superhumans or geniuses, but people....And what they may lack in perfection, God makes up for in love.*

A. Who would you list in a "Who's Who" of the five most outstanding men and women of the Bible other than Jesus? What strengths did each possess? What weaknesses did each possess? How was each person used to change the world?

B. How does God use our weaknesses for his purpose, according to 2 Corinthians 12:7-10 and 2 Corinthians 4?

C. If Satan were to try to convince you that you were of no special value to the Lord, how might he do it? How would you answer him?

2. *Look at the forgiveness found in those open arms and take courage.*

A. How do you picture God? Do you picture him with open arms?

B. As you read the following passages, make a list of the ways God's love and forgiveness for his followers is described: Exodus 34:6-7; Psalm 32; Psalm 103:1-18; Isaiah 44:21-22; 1 John 1:7-9.

C. Read again the description in Luke 15:20 of the father's reaction when he saw his son returning home. The next time you need to ask God's forgiveness, imagine him reacting to you in the same way—running to meet you, being filled with compassion, throwing his arms around you, and kissing you. What kind of courage does it take to talk to a father like that?

Chapter 23: A Street Vendor Named Contentment

1. *An hour of contentment. An hour when deadlines are forgotten and strivings have ceased. An hour when what we have overshadows what we want.*

A. How would you define contentment? How is it different from happiness? What is necessary in order to be content?

B. Read Philippians 4:11-13 where Paul says he has found the secret of contentment in all circumstances. What was that secret? What kind of circumstances had Paul been in, according to 2 Corinthians 11:23-28?

C. How rare is contentment? What words would best describe most of us on a normal day: worried, hurried, busy, frustrated, tired, anxious, discouraged—or—peaceful, serene, content, happy, relaxed? What advice might Paul give us to increase our contentment?

2. *"People seem strangely proud of their ulcers and headaches."*

A. In what way is that a true statement for many people? What makes stress and pressure virtual hallmarks of success?

B. According to Luke 12:22-34, what should be the hallmarks of our lives in Christ? To what does Jesus compare us? What do we compare our lives to—a rat race, swimming with the sharks? What contrasts are evident?

C. What does your physical health tell you about your sense of peace and contentment? What does it say about your worry level? To what extent are you doctoring the symptoms instead of addressing the problem?

Chapter 24: Close to the Cross— But Far from Christ

1. *So close to the cross but so far from the Christ.*

A. In what ways are we like the soldiers at the foot of the cross? Where are our eyes focused—up on the crucified Son of God or down on our possessions? Like they, in what way are we calloused to the sight of the crucifixion?

B. In what ways do we focus on the trivialities of religion and ignore the heart of the matter? What did Jesus say in Matthew 23:23-24 to those who focused on the more trivial issues of religion? How does Micah 6:8 define the "heart of the matter"?

C. What issues do you see churches arguing and dividing over today that you think Jesus would consider "tithing mint and cumin"? What would you consider the "more important matters" to be today?

2. *What about you? Can you build a bridge? Toss a rope? Span a chasm? Pray for oneness?*

A. How much unity is possible among religious groups? To what extent can churches have differences and still be unified?

B. From what you see in Jesus' prayer in John 17:11, 20-23, what is the appropriate basis for unity in the church today?

C. What can we do as individuals to increase unity among believers? What could your church do to increase unity with other churches?

Chapter 25: The Fog of the Broken Heart

1. *Seeing God like this does wonders for our own suffering. God was never more human than at this hour. God was never nearer to us than when he hurt.*

A. How does it help to understand that Jesus in his humanity suffered in the Garden of Gethsemane?

B. Reread the account in Mark 14:32-42 or in one of the other Gospels. What about Jesus' behavior seems very "human" to you? What about these events is surprising?

C. If this were the only passage available to a non-Christian, what basic principles of the gospel could be taught from it? In what way can this passage serve as an example and as encouragement when you pray amidst the "fog"?

2. *If it is true that in suffering God is most like man, maybe in our suffering we can see God like never before.*

A. In times of suffering, is your vision of God better or worse? Under what circumstances do you turn to God? Under what circumstances do you turn away from him?

B. How do the following passages assure us that God not only understands but cares about our sufferings: Matthew 10:28-31; John 14:1-3; Romans 8:28-39?

C. How can times of suffering ultimately be a blessing? Read 2 Corinthians 4:7—5:11; 2 Thessalonians 1:3-10; and Luke 6:20-22.

Chapter 26: Pão, Senhor?

1. *Living in Brazil, one has daily opportunities to buy a candy bar or sandwich for these little outcasts. It's the least one can do.*

A. Have you ever had an experience like Max's? What do you do when you are confronted by a beggar, the homeless, a request for a donation from a charity?

B. How did Jesus say we were to treat others in Matthew 10:40-42 and Matthew 25:31-46? What did James say about it in James 2:14-17?

C. How would you summarize the commands embodied in the above passages? What kind of rationalizations can most easily keep Christians from actually doing what we are told to do?

2. *If I am so moved by a street orphan who says thank you for a piece of bread, how much more is God moved when I pause to thank him—really thank him—for saving my soul?*

A. Do we sometimes take our blessings, and particularly our salvation, for granted? Why?

B. What do the following passages teach about expressing gratitude toward God: 1 Thessalonians 5:16-18; Ephesians 5:19-20; Colossians 1:10-14; Colossians 3:15-17? For what are we to give thanks? When?

C. To what extent are praise and gratitude a part of your prayers? How do they compare to your petitions to God? When was the last time you truly thanked God for saving your soul?

Chapter 27: Puppies, Butterflies and a Savior

1. *Guilt creeps in on cat's paws and steals whatever joy might have flickered in our eyes.*

A. Max compares guilt to a cat stealing our joy. What other ways could you describe guilt's effects?

B. How do these scriptures describe the effects of guilt: Psalm 31:9-10; Psalm 38; Psalm 51? What insights do they offer into the cure for guilt?

C. Can joy exist alongside guilt? Which is the stronger emotion? What advice would you give for replacing guilt with peace and joy?

2. *Quit trying to quench your own guilt. You can't do it. There's no way. Not with a bottle of whiskey or perfect Sunday School attendance.*

A. How do we try to quench the feelings of guilt? How do we try to rationalize it away?

B. In your own words explain the message of the following verses: Isaiah 43:25; 1 John 1:7-9; Hebrews 10:22.

C. When is guilt a necessary and healthy emotion? When is guilt an unhealthy emotion? When is it unhealthy not to feel guilt? How would you summarize what part guilt plays in the Christian's life?

Chapter 28: God's Testimony

1. *I thought of his faith, his ability to believe, and his surprise that there were some who couldn't.*

A. Generally speaking, who has an easier time believing—those who have a little education or those who have a lot of education? What potential dangers are there in being too "sophisticated" in knowledge?

B. What do Romans 1:18-20 and Acts 14:15-17 teach about people's ability to see the existence of God?

C. Restate in your own words the definition of faith in Hebrews 11:1-3.

D. Which is harder for you to believe—that there is a God or that there isn't? How would you explain your reasons for faith to someone who didn't believe in God?

2. *To really understand and believe in the miracle on the cross, we'd do well to witness God's miracles every day.*

A. What daily evidence of God's presence is most compelling to you? Does it ever become so commonplace that you take it for granted?

B. What evidences of God does the psalmist celebrate in Psalm 19:1-4 and Psalm 33:6-15?

C. If you were to write a psalm about the daily miracles of God, what miracles would you include?

Chapter 29: Dynamite Decisions

1. *One statement made by our master offers two basic tools for keeping our cool in the heat of a decision. "Watch and pray so that you will not fall into temptation."*

A. Have you ever been in the "garden of decision" yourself? In what way has your loyalty been challenged? When you are suddenly faced with a decision, how do you tend to react?

B. Reread the account in Mark 14:32-52 of the garden scene. How do we see Jesus using these tools? What was the result? What was the result of the disciples not using them?

C. How would you restate the following passages in modern terms: Proverbs 4:23-27; 1 Corinthians 16:13; 1 Peter 5:8?

D. It is said that a person's character is revealed in moments of crisis. What specific suggestions can you make for preparing ahead of time so that a Christ-like character is revealed in moments of crisis and sudden decisions?

2. *Second tool: "Pray." Prayer isn't telling God anything new. There is not a sinner nor a saint who would surprise him. What prayer does is invite God to walk the shadowy pathways of life with us.*

A. Do you agree with Max's statements on prayer? How could you expand on the idea that it invites God to walk with us?

B. Read Luke 18:1-8. What lesson is Jesus teaching about prayer? What additional insights into prayer do these verses offer: Ephesians 6:18; Colossians 4:2-4; Hebrews 4:16? For what are we to pray? What is to be our attitude in prayer?

C. What specific things are you praying for in regard to yourself? What specific things are you praying for in regard to others? In what other areas might you want to invite God to walk with you?

Chapter 30: What Did You Expect?

1. *Expectations. They create conditional love.*

A. What is the problem with conditional love? What does it do to marriages? to children? to faith?

B. In what way did Jesus fail to meet the people's expectations of the Messiah? What did the people expect him to do? According to Matthew 11:1-6 and John 6:35-66, how did even those close to Jesus have wrong expectations? What happened when their expectations were not met?

C. What expectations do we have of Jesus? What happens when he fails to meet our expectations? For instance, what happens to your faith and love for Jesus when he fails to answer a prayer as you expect?

2. *Jesus couched his expectations with two important companions. Forgiveness and acceptance.*

A. Within this study what are some examples of Jesus' expectations not being met? How did he respond? Take, for example, the disciples in the Garden of Gethsemane.

B. Look at these instances in which people did not meet Jesus' expectations: the disciples (Matthew 17:14-21; Mark 8:1-21); Judas (Matthew 26:47-50); Peter (Matthew 16:21-23). In each case, what did Jesus expect of them, why did people fail to meet his expectations, and how did he treat them?

C. Spend some time in prayer, asking forgiveness for failing to meet Jesus' expectations of you and praising him for accepting you despite your failures. Also pray for the strength to be more Christ-like in forgiving and accepting others who fail to meet your expectations.

Chapter 31: Come Home

1. *When pride meets hunger, a human will do things that were before unthinkable.*

A. Do you agree with Max that, given the right circumstances, "a human will do things that were before unthinkable"? To what degree are each of us capable of the most heinous sins?

B. How would you describe humanity's condition—basically good, basically evil, a product of the environment, a product of genetics? What do the following passages teach about the sinfulness of humanity: Ecclesiastes 7:20; Isaiah 64:6; Romans 3:9-23?

C. Why is it good for each of us to recognize our sinfulness? How does it affect our perspective on Christ's sacrifice for us? How does it affect our understanding and forgiveness of other people?

2. *"Whatever you have done, whatever you have become, it doesn't matter. Please come home."*

A. In what way does Jesus make the same statement to us?

B. For you, which images in the following passages best illustrate a sinner's journey and homecoming: Deuteronomy 4:29-31; Deuteronomy 30; Luke 15:3-10? How do they describe the sinner's attitude? How do they describe God's reception?

C. Describe a special homecoming you have experienced. What memories of it are most vivid? If an earthly homecoming can be so powerful, can you imagine what a heavenly homecoming is like?

Chapter 32: Consistent Inconsistencies

1. *Evil is paradoxically close to goodness.*

A. What examples can you give of Max's statement? Ministers dedicated to their flock but neglecting their family? Friendship becoming an affair? A desire for "good works" denying God's grace?

B. The Bible is full of examples of good intentions leading to evil results and evil intentions masquerading as good. How were the Pharisees caught up in this paradox? Read Matthew 23:1-12, 15, 23-24, 27-28. How had good become perverted into evil? According to 2 Corinthians 11:13-15, how does evil masquerade as good?

C. How can we discern good from evil, according to 1 John 4:1-3 and Romans 12? Make a list of the practical indicators of the godly life listed in Romans 12.

2. *Never did what is right involve itself so intimately with what is wrong, as it did when Jesus was suspended between heaven and earth.*

A. How was the crucifixion the greatest, and ultimate, battle between good and evil? In what way were good and evil closely connected?

B. Look back at Matthew's account of the crucifixion, beginning with 26:1 and ending with 27:56. Draw a line vertically down a piece of paper and on the left side list the significant nouns and verbs within that reading that describe the forces of wrong that precipitated the crucifixion. On the right side of the line list the nouns and verbs that describe Jesus during those events.

C. How do you react to that list? In one sentence summarize the message of the list. In what way is it the message of this book? In what way is it the message of the Bible itself?

Chapter 33: The Roar

1. *Over half of the world has yet to hear the story of the Messiah, much less study it.*

A. What opportunities are there to take the story to places in the world where it has previously been denied? What is your church doing to take advantage of these opportunities?

B. How would you answer those who believe they are not articulate enough to present the gospel? What encouragement is found in 1 Corinthians 1:20—2:5; Romans 1:16-17; Ephesians 1:13-14; Colossians 1:3-6?

C. What are the essential matters in telling the story of the Messiah? What is not essential?

2. *Maybe we all need to witness his majesty and sigh at his victory. Maybe we need to hear our own commission again.*

A. In what way is this a fitting chapter to conclude the book? In your opinion, what was Max's purpose in writing this book? For you, has it been achieved? What is your response to the Savior he has presented?

B. What is the commission that Jesus gave in Matthew 28:18-20? Why is it often called the "Great Commission"? What are we commissioned to do in Romans 10:9-17?

C. How are you participating in taking the story of the Messiah to those who have not heard it? What could you do to be more actively involved? Could 1 Corinthians 9:16 become your marching orders?

D. At the beginning of this study you wrote five goals for the study. Look at those goals again. To what extent have you accomplished them? Are there ones that you would like to continue to pursue?

God's Assurance:
His Word

If you prayed this prayer,
The Bible Says...

**"For 'whoever calls upon the name of the Lord will be saved.'"
Romans 10:13**

Did you sincerely ask Jesus Christ to come into your life? Where is He right now? What has He given you?

"For it is by grace you have been saved, through faith—and this is not from yourselves, it is the gift of God—not by works, so that no one can boast." Ephesians 2:8,9

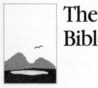

The
Bible Says...

"He who has the Son has life; he who does not have the Son of God does not have life. These things I have written to you who believe in the name of the Son of God, that you may know that you have eternal life, and that you may continue to believe in the name of the Son of God." 1 John 5:12–13, NKJV

Receiving Christ, we are born into God's family through the supernatural work of the Holy Spirit who indwells every believer...this is called regeneration or the "new birth."

This is just the beginning of a wonderful new life in Christ. To deepen this relationship you should:

1. Read your Bible every day to know Christ better.
2. Talk to God in prayer every day.
3. Tell others about Christ.
4. Worship, fellowship, and serve with other Christians in a church where Christ is preached.
5. As Christ's representative in a needy world, demonstrate your new life by your love and concern for others.

God bless you as you do.

Billy Graham

If you want further help in the decision you have made, write to:
Billy Graham Evangelistic Association P.O. Box 779, Minneapolis, Minnesota 55440-0779

Step 1 | God's Purpose: Peace and Life

God loves you and wants you to experience peace and life—abundant and eternal.

The Bible Says . . .

". . . we have peace with God through our Lord Jesus Christ." Romans 5:1

"For God so loved the world that He gave His only begotten Son, that whoever believes in Him should not perish but have everlasting life." John 3:16

". . . I have come that they may have life, and that they may have it more abundantly." John 10:10b

Since God planned for us to have peace and the abundant life right now, why are most people not having this experience?

Step 2 | Our Problem: Separation

God created us in His own image to have an abundant life. He did not make us as robots to automatically love and obey Him, but gave us a will and a freedom of choice.

We chose to disobey God and go our own willful way. We still make this choice today. This results in separation from God.

Our choice results in separation from God.

The Bible Says . . .

"For all have sinned and fall short of the glory of God." Romans 3:23

"For the wages of sin is death, but the gift of God is eternal life in Christ Jesus our Lord." Romans 6:23

People (Sinful)   God (Holy)

Our Attempts

Through the ages, individuals have tried in many ways to bridge this gap . . . without success . . .

The Bible Says . . .

"There is a way that seems right to man, but in the end it leads to death." Proverbs 14:12

"But your iniquities have separated you from God; and your sins have hidden His face from you, so that He will not hear." Isaiah 59:2

There is only one remedy for this problem of separation.

Step 3 # God's Remedy: The Cross

Jesus Christ is the only answer to this problem. He died on the Cross and rose from the grave, paying the penalty for our sin and bridging the gap between God and people.

The Bible Says . . .

". . . God is on one side and all the people on the other side, and Christ Jesus, Himself man, is between them to bring them together . . ." 1 Timothy 2:5

"For Christ also has suffered once for sins, the just for the unjust, that He might bring us to God . . ." 1 Peter 3:18a

"But God demonstrates His own love for us in this: While we were still sinners, Christ died for us." Romans 5:8

God has provided the only way . . . we must make the choice . . .

Step 4 Our Response:
Receive Christ

We must trust Jesus Christ and receive Him by personal invitation.

The Bible Says . . .

"**Behold, I stand at the door and knock. If anyone hears My voice and opens the door, I will come in to him and dine with him, and he with Me.**" **Revelation 3:20**

"**But as many as received Him, to them He gave the right to become children of God, even to those who believe in His name.**" **John 1:12**

"**. . . if you confess with your mouth the Lord Jesus and believe in your heart that God has raised Him from the dead, you will be saved.**" **Romans 10:9**

Are you here . . . or here?

Is there any good reason why you cannot receive Jesus Christ right now?

How to receive Christ:

1. Admit your need (I am a sinner).
2. Be willing to turn from your sins (repent).
3. Believe that Jesus Christ died for you on the Cross and rose from the grave.
4. Through prayer, invite Jesus Christ to come in and control your life through the Holy Spirit. (Receive Him as Lord and Savior.)

What to Pray:

Dear Lord Jesus,

   I know that I am a sinner and need Your forgiveness. I believe that You died for my sins. I want to turn from my sins. I now invite You to come into my heart and life. I want to trust and follow You as Lord and Savior.

In Jesus' name. Amen.

_____   _____
        Date   Signature